THE STREET MARKETS OF LONDON

PHOTOGRAPHS BY
L. MOHOLY-NAGY

THE
STREET
MARKETS
OF
LONDON

TEXT BY
MARY BENEDETTA

REISSUED 1972
BY
BENJAMIN BLOM INC.
PUBLISHERS
NEW YORK

First published London, 1936
Reissued 1972 by
Benjamin Blom, Inc.
New York, N.Y. 10025

Library of Congress
Catalog Card Number 72-84542

Printed in the
United States of America

Contents

Foreword

By L. MOHOLY-NAGY

THE Photographer can scarcely find a more fascinating task than that of providing a pictorial record of modern city life. London's street markets present him with an opportunity of this kind. It is not, however, a task to which the purely æsthetic principle of pictorial composition—which many readers may expect in my work—can be applied, for from its very nature it requires the use of the pictorial sequence and thus of a more effective technique approximating to that of the film. I am convinced that the days of the merely "beautiful" photograph are numbered and that we shall be increasingly interested in providing a truthful record of objectively determined fact.

To many peoples' minds the street market still suggests romantic notions of showmen, unorganised trade, bargains and the sale of stolen goods. The photographic report can either encourage or correct these ideas. I consider the latter to be the more important task, since in my opinion these markets are primarily to be regarded as a social necessity, the shopping-centre, in fact, for a large part of the working-class.

The subject is a vast one, comprising problems of history, sociology, economics and town planning. It is approached in this book by means of literary and impressionistic photo-reportage. This method of studying a fragment of present-day reality from a social and economic point of view has a wide general appeal. The text provides considerable oppor-

vii

tunities for this study and it was my aim to underline these opportunities through the pictorial record.

For those interested in the technical aspects of photography I should add that as a rule I prefer to work with a large camera in order to obtain the minutely graded black-white-grey photo-values of the contact print, impossible to achieve in enlargements. But unfortunately the large camera is much too clumsy for taking rapid shots without being observed. The whole street immediately crowds around the photographer, the natural life of the scene is paralysed and the characteristic features of the traders, their happy-go-lucky behaviour, their elementary actor's skill, their impetuosity, are lost.

Thus after several attempts with a large camera I always returned to the Leica, with which one can work rapidly, unobserved and—even in the London atmosphere, or in interiors—with a reliable degree of precision.

I hope, therefore, that many a defect incompatible with the standard of photographic quality I have so often demanded in theory will be condoned by the reader, in view of the rapid and unprepared fixation of lively scenes that could never have been posed.   L. MOHOLY-NAGY.

PHOTOGRAPHS BY
L. MOHOLY-NAGY

Petticoat Lane: General View

Petticoat Lane: The Spectacle Man

Petticoat Lane: In a side street. Some Arabian
visitors at a second-hand clothes stall

Petticoat Lane: Umbrella stall

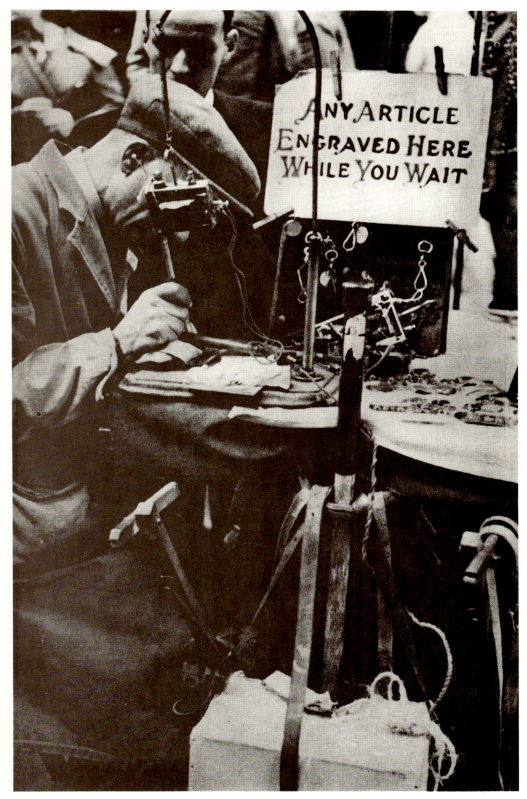

Petticoat Lane: An engraver

Petticoat Lane: Alf, the Purse King

Petticoat Lane: The wealth of a trinket stall

Petticoat Lane: The Glass Man's burly auctioneer

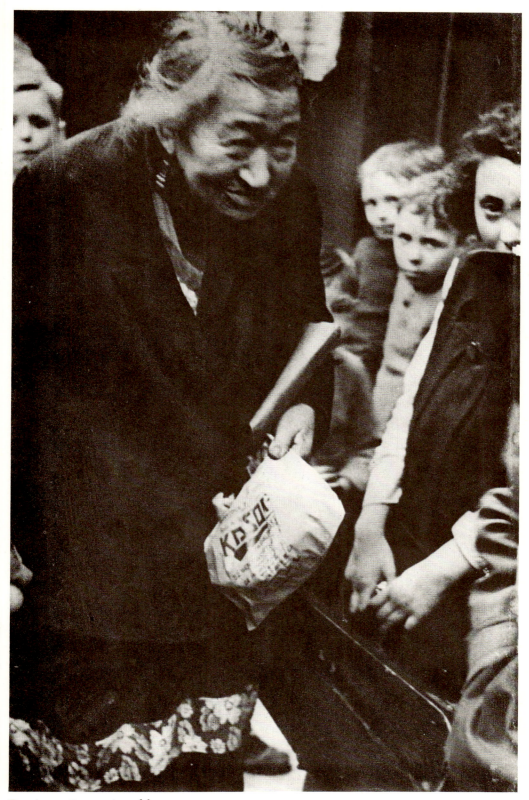

Petticoat Lane: An old customer

Petticoat Lane: The man's "store"

Petticoat Lane: A bad day. Waiting for customers

Petticoat Lane: Second-hand shoes

Farringdon Street: "There is one tragic figure in the group"

Petticoat Lane: "Pick me out two soft roes," she says

Berwick Street: A family business—Flower sellers

Caledonian Market: "Go down with an empty larder . . ."

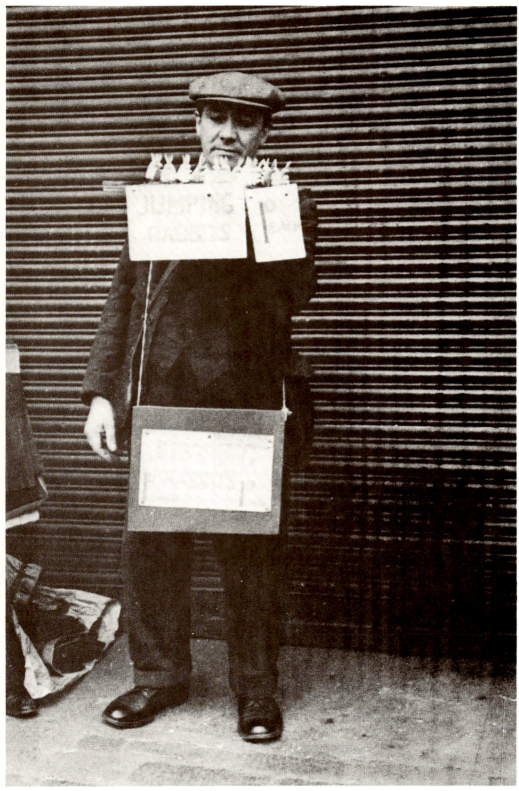

Brixton: Another sort of Rabbit Man

Petticoat Lane: " . . . The sound that only wet fish can make"

Choumert Road: "I only got one cat"

North End Road: A character study

Petticoat Lane: "Nobody makes them nowadays,
and they might be worth buying . . ."

Billingsgate: Fish ready for the stalls

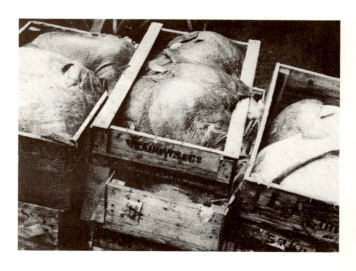

Berwick Market: "There you can get thin
pure silk stockings for 1s. 3d."

Berwick Market: General view

Covent Garden: Waiting for a bargain

Covent Garden: Who said women were gossips?

Kentish Town: "We 'ave a salad barrel as well . . ."

Petticoat Lane: "You must never be shocked in a street market"

Shepherd's Bush: "A gypsy-like woman in fancy dress"

Petticoat Lane: An Oriental perfume seller

Shepherd's Bush: The Medicine Man

Petticoat Lane: "A man who sells a mysterious preparation for making brass fenders look like chromium"

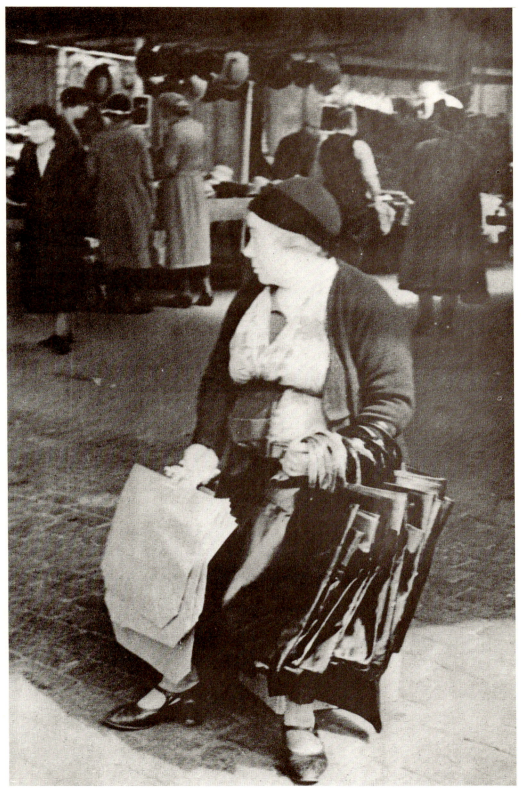

Caledonian Market: Bags to hold the bargains

Caledonian Market: Cool drinks for weary shoppers

Covent Garden: A rest from shelling peas

Camden Town: Music on a home-made instrument

Petticoat Lane: Still life in enamel

Petticoat Lane: "Saturday afternoon when all
the children are out of school"

North Road: "A nice, kind face"

Hillmerton Road: Cheap face towels

A Clash With The Police

Commercial Road: Ties and scarves

Brick Lane: Second-hand? No, but they might be third-hand

Caledonian Market: North Road entrance

Caledonian Market: "They have no stalls, but
spread them out on the ground"

Caledonian Market: Fox-hunting

Caledonian Market: "The gentleman of the next department . . ."

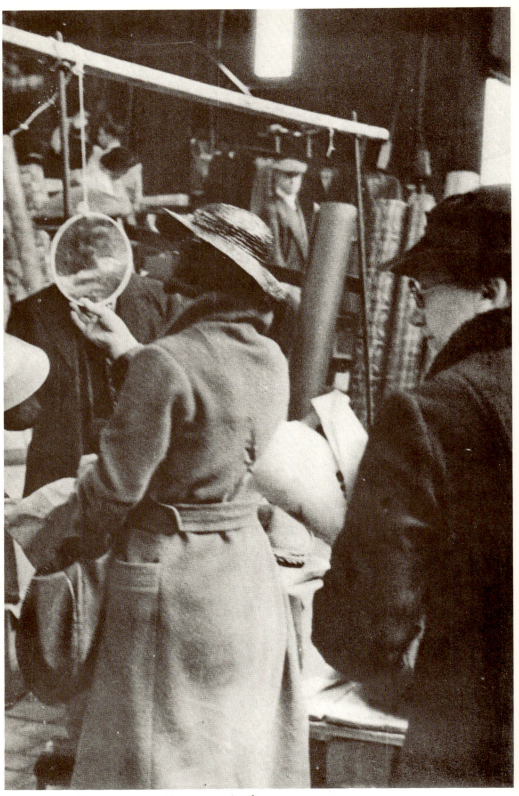

Caledonian Market: A well-equipped "fitting-room"

Caledonian Market: "The pages were a bit shaky in places"

Caledonian Market: Youth at the stall

Caledonian Market: The old farmer comes to town

Caledonian Market: General view

Caledonian Market: "Where you can find what you want for less money"

Caledonian Market: Specialist in outsizes

Caledonian Market: "The Silver Kings'
stalls are the centre of attraction"

Caledonian Market: "He is an artist, and had a
picture hung in the Academy in 1917"

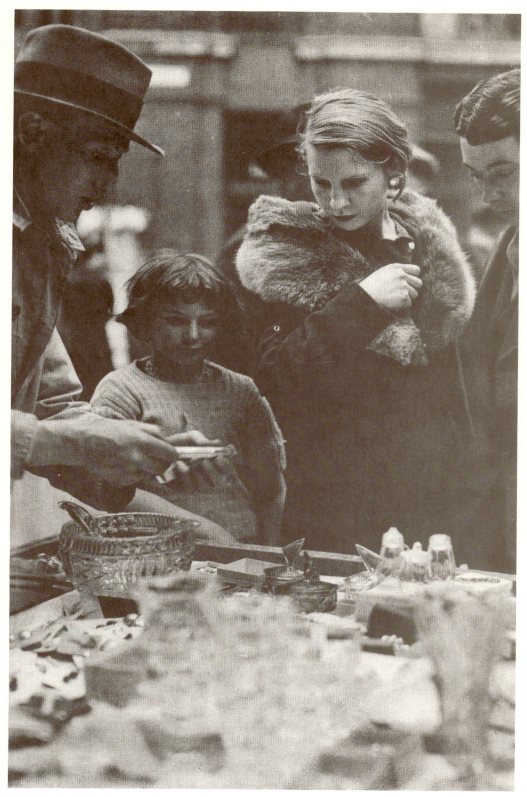

Caledonian Market: "Whatever happens, you are sure to enjoy it"

Commercial Road: Stall for housewives

Billingsgate: General view

Covent Garden: At the market

Billingsgate: Study in concentration

Billingsgate: Getting busy

Billingsgate: A fish porter in the traditional and practical hat

Billingsgate: Where you find every age and every type

Petticoat Lane

PETTICOAT LANE! Here is a real pantomime of life. Some of the quaintest personalities trade in this market, and eighty per cent. of the wares are said to be genuine. The market is only open on Sunday mornings, when "the Lane" becomes the busiest street in London.

Take an early train to Aldgate Station, for you must be there by ten o'clock to view the wares. Turn to the right when you come out of the station, and then the first turning to the right is Petticoat Lane.

At ten o'clock nearly two hundred stalls have been put up, and the cheap-jacks are hanging out their wares. Everything comes out of an incredible collection of boxes and tins. In the twinkling of an eye each rickety stall is simply smothered with myriads of things—so many it seems in danger of collapse.

It is while they are decking their stalls that you can sometimes speak to the sellers. And there are some very charming people in Petticoat Lane.

There is old Heyday, with his silver hair, rosy cheeks, and his gentle, courtly manners. He sells rubber stamps. You write on a piece of paper what you would like to have on your rubber stamp, and pay him a shilling. A few days later along it comes by post, for he has to make it for you at home.

His other line is spectacles—yes, just spectacles. What kind? "Reading spectacles." The Petticoat Lane shoppers have no optician. If their eyesight grows dim they go to Mr. Heyday and choose a frame. Then they search among a bundle of lenses until they find two that suit them—and two alike. Then, of course, they bargain with him.

Heyday's quiet manner is a curious contrast to the raucous cries that go on all round him. He does not shout or invite you to buy. Sometimes he says very quietly, "Rubber stamps," while he turns them over rather tenderly, and looks critically at his handiwork.

I asked Heyday what he did the rest of the week.

"I go round to the other markets," he said, "and in harvest-time I go to the village markets all round Norwich and various parts of Norfolk. Rubber stamps," he added gently to the assembling crowd. And I went to look at some statues.

You can get a plaster statue nearly two feet high for a shilling. And you can buy a set—a clock and two vases for 7s. 6d. or less. All these statues come from a factory in Highbury, so they arrive brand-new. Their salesman is a cheery young man called Joe Wilkins. Joe is a greengrocer the rest of the week, and he is one of the youngest salesmen in Petticoat Lane.

"Bob each," he calls cheerily, "Alsatians, monkeys, elephants, donkeys, cats—all a bob each."

Some of the stalls sell new afternoon dresses for 5s. Later in the morning you can get one for less. The kind of dress that would cost 35s. to £2 in a shop. The men's clothes are prolific, both new and second-hand. People come on a cold day, buy an overcoat, and walk off in it. Fifty-shilling tailors are not in it at Petticoat Lane. You walk off "posh" for far less than that. There is one man who draws quite a crowd by being his own mannequin and talking salesman. Any actor might envy the speed with which he effects a change when he is going to show off another suit.

Say "Knife" to Mrs. Cohen, and she will supply you with anything from a murderous-looking carver to a dainty fruit knife, and she has plenty of whole new sets at bargain prices. These are not second-hand, they all come from the same factory and are really good quality. Mrs. Cohen herself is a friendly, pleasant person with a housewifely knowledge about knives. She has a complete programme of markets all the week, except on Wednesday, which is her rest day.

Eleven-thirty, and the market scene is at its height. Petti-

2

coat Lane echoes with shouts and cries. Bells ring, alarm clocks go off, and voices grow hoarse in the desperate competition to be heard.

Crowds edge their way along the pavements behind the stalls, and a dense crowd moves slowly up and down in the road in the centre. Every other second they stop and stare, or some one shouts a bid. Sometimes they get hung up by a clever salesman, and there is a jam that lasts for twenty minutes. That is generally the point where somebody tries to get through with a perambulator.

But it is not an unruly crowd—rather very orderly and very quiet. They are too busy watching and listening to give any trouble. It is best to keep to the pavements behind the stalls as there is more chance of getting close. You may miss a great deal by being in the middle of the road, even though the pavement is "the wrong side of the counter."

No feminine eye can resist a bargain in stockings. There is a man in "the Lane" who sells nothing but stockings. You cannot miss him, because of the way he decorates his hat. Several pound notes and ten-shilling notes are tied round the crown with a piece of string, and he suffers many taunts of "Hi! lend us yer hat a second," or "How much'll yer take fer yer hat?"

He calls himself "The Pound Note Man" and keeps up a vigorous chatter all the time. "Look here," he cries, taking up a bundle of stockings and slapping them loudly, "Look here, only a penny a pair. One dozen pairs for a shilling. Now look here, I'll tell you what I'll do—— This is only once I'm doing it. All these pairs for a penny a pair—— Look here, I'll tell you what I'll do——"

Some of his stockings are a wonderful bargain.

At another stall you stop and look at the wares. You had not noticed the man eyeing you from behind the improvised counter.

"Well, if you don't want to buy, what *do* yer want. Lay off hanging around my stall."

3

Well, never mind. You half expected that might happen.
Otherwise it would never have been a proper market day.
And you get lost in the crowd as quickly as a pickpocket.

There is a very rough-and-ready foot clinic on one stall.
People sit on a table having their corns cured for a few pence.
And the crowd watches.

Rather curiously there is a food-stall close to the foot clinic.
The herbalist has a stall with anything from senna-pods to
leaves from a juniper tree. You can tell him you have indi-
gestion and watch him make up a cure for it. His assistant
will show you "a genuine Norwegian fir cone." Nobody
quarrels over its origin.

Policemen in uniform move through the crowd all the
time. The L.C.C. inspector goes from stall to stall with his
plain-clothes assistant, checking the stall-holders' licences.

Sometimes you are almost beaten back by waves of over-
powering perfume. Scents and hair-oils are something more
than exotic in Petticoat Lane, but people can have their own
scents made up specially for them in true Bond Street style.
Customers to the barber's shop enjoy the same glaring pub-
licity as the corn sufferers. And the barber gives a free whiff
of hair oil to the front row of the audience.

Tom Bookman calls himself an "umbrella specialist," and
underneath on the worn brass plate is written, "established
on this spot since 1873." Unquestionably there are bargains
among the umbrellas. For 2s. or less you can get an umbrella
that would go with very smart clothes.

People sell a curious combination of things on the same
stall. One cheap-jack sells razors and footballs, and he has
some quite good razors for 2d. and 3d. each. You can get
bargains in cigarette-lighters in this market, and the man
who sells them to you will also fill them with petrol without
extra charge. Some well-known manufacturers of suit-cases
have a stall there for selling off old stock. Enormous boxes
of chocolates are sold by a kind of quick-fire auction that
almost takes your breath away.

4

There may have been something you envied in the window of a West End store. Later you might see it in Petticoat Lane. That has happened to me, and this time it cost 1s. instead of 15s. 6d. It was a particular kind of reading-lamp, with a self-contained battery. I felt it was an indulgence to pay 15s. 6d. for it, but at 1s. it became a bargain and therefore excusable.

Nobody could despise the perfect little knitted sets of baby-clothes that Petticoat Lane has to offer for a top price of 4s., which probably means a bargain for 1s. 6d. or 2s. If you have a dog, meet Mr. J. Park, who will engrave your dog collar for you on the spot. He does it perfectly—and all for 1s. You can have a ring engraved by him as well.

"There are lots of common people down 'the Lane.' I'm the only respectable one," called a hoarse voice. It came from a very tough-looking individual behind a clothing-stall.

"I'll give four bob to any one who wants to dash it on the ground," yelled an old man trying to sell a glass bowl.

One of the most entertaining characters in "the Lane" is Mike Stern. Mike has his stall on a side-road, and he seems to do bigger business than any one. Not long ago he broadcast in the "In Town To-night" programme, and later appeared in the "Radiolympia" exhibition. So now he still advertises the fact on his name-board.

Whatever you do, you must not miss him. He stands high up on the platform inside his big stall, crying his wares in a lively witty patter, while his assistants take the bids and wrap up parcels like lightning. His trousers are bright scarlet, and he has a checked shirt, patterned in great big squares. And on top of this he generally wears one or two things he is trying to sell. I saw him wearing a housekeeper's apron and a baby's bonnet. Mike is a born entertainer as well as a salesman.

"Here you are now—nice bunch of handkerchiefs, seventy-two blows on one handkerchief. You can blow yer brains out for a shilling. There you are now—two little ones in free for

5

the old woman. Now some tablecloths. Last two I've got. Only half a crown the pair. That's right, send 'em along. Here we are—another last two . . ."

Furs are always problematical, and they become much more so in Petticoat Lane. But if you know enough about them you can sometimes pick up bargains in quite good skins.

Jewellery needs very careful management—but you can get it, certainly. There are solid gold watches, and valuable rings and brooches, but you will need your keenest wits to do some really courageous bargaining. They will not make it easy for you. Highly valuable jewels have been discovered in Petticoat Lane and bought for a mere song.

Collectors of antique silver should never overlook this market. There are sometimes things you could not buy elsewhere for love or money, and there are nearly always some really lovely silver candlesticks waiting to be bought for a few shillings.

One of the most romantic stalls in the market is a stall of old musical instruments kept by Isidore Michael. I could have lingered there for hours. When you want to buy a violin you need not go to an expensive music-shop and pay pounds for it. Michael can sell you a really lovely old fiddle for 5s. There are all kinds of instruments on his stall, from mandolins to zither harps, trumpets, and tenor banjos. He buys them up from pawn-brokers, and there are chances of picking up valuable finds.

Michael himself can play about half a dozen different instruments. He speaks in a quiet, rather educated voice, and he does not shout his wares or trouble you to buy.

Instead he picks up an instrument now and again and plays a few bars of some haunting little melody. He has the touch of a musician. You can study each instrument as much as you like—if he sees you are careful how you handle them.

All the time the crowd ambles along, watching and waiting. They are waiting till the end of the morning, when the cheap-jacks will begin letting their things go for less—and

6

less. Like them you must keep the things you like best in your memory, and then join in the final frenzied bidding at the end.

Petticoat Lane needs very many visits—and even then you will want to go again.

Leather Lane

LEATHER LANE is the lunch-time market. Clerks and office-boys revel in it, and sometimes if you keep your eyes open you will see "the boss" steal down its pavements to look for a bargain.

Holborn Circus is such a maelstrom of hurry and bustle that Leather Lane stays unnoticed—except by those who know it. Yet, sandwiched between a dark-red pseudo-Gothic building and Gamage's stores, there is a narrow street that holds one of the oldest street markets in London. Long ago it was the liveliest street in the district and attracted all the people. Since then the pseudo-Gothic building has reared its ugly head and tried to hide it, while the huge stores at its very entrance can provide everything for millions of homes. But Leather Lane struggles bravely on and refuses to be crushed. In spite of everything it has kept its pride—like the old lady who rides through the streets in a dilapidated family coach, while her bearing makes all the people in the motor-cars seem vulgar and stupid. And like the old lady it brings a lump to our throat, for there is something very sad about it.

That is one aspect of Leather Lane. The other is a happy one, for it has so many genuinely honest people in it, and an air of respectability that makes you feel as safe and contented as you do with your favourite local tradespeople. This sounds incredible with our normal conception of a street market, but if you became one of its regular customers you would soon find it was true.

There are many people working in Holborn whose hours begin before the shops open and finish after they are closed. Their lunch-time is too short for a voyage to a shopping centre—besides, their "budget" could not spare the extra fares. So they find refuge and all they want in Leather Lane.

9

The best feature is the fruit. Whatever the time of year, there is always plenty of it and very cheap. What is more, it all looks very tempting. You do not see dried-up oranges or withering bananas. When you only buy one apple or one banana you would expect it to be quite perfect. And that is what you *can* do in Leather Lane. You can buy one of anything if you like. Nobody tries to force you to buy a pound of apples when you just wanted one to chew behind a door in the office.

Perhaps a shopping housewife might say, "Yes, but I couldn't buy fruit off an open stall. Just think of all the people who've handled it!" But then no fruit was ever harmed by being washed before it goes into the dessert bowl, and for all anybody knows the market fruit has probably had far less handling than it would in the shops. In any case, there are many spotlessly clean hands behind the stalls in Leather Lane, and the grapes are handled just as tenderly as they are by the chef at the Ritz.

Close to the far end of the market, going away from Holborn Circus, is the fruit-stall kept by Mrs. Kingham. She has a wonderful display of good fruit, and there is a kind little heart inside her small body. One of the best times to visit her stall is just before Christmas. In a time when the shops are displaying boxes of tangerines for 2s. and 2s. 6d. a dozen, Mrs. Kingham will sell you lovely ones for three a penny, and less. All fruit becomes expensive at this time, but not in Leather Lane, and nobody takes advantage of "the Christmas spirit" by putting up their prices.

Mrs. Kingham's voice is gentle and sad, and she mothers her customers with an almost heartrending sympathy.

"Can't do it, dear, can't do it. That holly cost me too much money."

She almost cries over her inability to charge a customer the penny less they want to pay.

I saw an old woman come up to her and ask the price of a bunch of mistletoe. It was twopence and more than she

10

could afford, so she turned away with a set expression and hovered hopelessly beside the neighbouring stall. Mrs. Kingham's large liquid eyes followed her commiseratingly, "I'll have some cheaper later on, Mother," she called after the retreating figure.

Then came a young woman who was buying giddily for Christmas, her arms laden with parcels and her cheeks glowing with excitement. She bought a huge Christmas-tree for 9d., the size many of us have paid 10s. for and thought we were lucky.

It was then that the parcels became troublesome and toppled down on the rain-soaked pavement. Sympathising volubly, Mrs. Kingham rushed to the rescue and produced a helpful piece of string from round her neck.

String is an uncertainty in Leather Lane, but there is plenty of newspaper. An old man comes round and distributes it about half-past eleven, and if there is a shortage he promises a further supply in half-an-hour's time.

There is a bespectacled young salesman called William Read, whose stall is at the Holborn Circus end of the market. He is another person with good fruit for sale, but just before Christmas he substitutes the fruit for Christmas cards, which he sells on commission.

George Roberts sells nothing but braces, trouser belts, and men's suspenders, all at bargain prices. If there are any humbling disasters to a man's braces while he is at the office, they can always be rectified in Leather Lane.

One of the most striking things about Leather Lane is its comparative quietness. Few people call out their wares, and still more seldom do they try and "draw the crowd."

There is a dashing young Spaniard, called Mecados, who holds a spirited auction with tins of toffee and boxes of chocolates. The office-boys watch him admiringly—he is like the hero of dozens of adventure stories—and the tins of toffee go like lightning. Toffee that is normally 8d. a quarter is sold at 2s. for a four-pound tin.

11

I expected every minute to see him as a Spanish buccaneer or a mediæval bull-fighter, and I blinked my eyes hard to remind myself I was in a street market. He stands out vividly among his more stolid companions, and he has a Fairbanks smile that flashes on the toffee-buyers as he hands them their tins. There is life in Leather Lane while Mecados holds his court.

Do you want a pair of opera-glasses which normally cost £3? You can buy them at James Carroll's stall for 2s. 6d. to 4s. 6d., "with cases and straps," as he tells you in his quiet voice.

Another tremendous feature of the market besides fruit, is the variety of parts of wireless sets, electrical fittings, and batteries—everything that delights the eyes of young men and boys. And they can get them very cheaply. There are several stalls devoted entirely to these things, so the demand seems to be unquestioned.

There is one stall, kept by a man who conceals his name, that sells rows of curious-looking inventions called "flashers." They are sets of coloured bulbs that wink all the time, like the lights you see outside shops and cinemas. People buy "flashers" when they cannot afford expensive advertisement lighting, for they only cost 2s. 6d. each.

The person to have a talk with is Joe Wiltshire, who keeps a stall for pots of plants and flowering shrubs. Joe has been in Leather Lane over thirty years, and his mother was there all her lifetime before him.

Old Mrs. Wiltshire does not appear very often now, because her limbs are getting too old to stay far from the fireside, but she cannot resist coming back now and then to see how things are going on. Joe is a delightful person to meet, and he has a round, red, cheery face and the nicest nature you could find.

His stall is a real temptation. You can go there in the worst week in the year for plants and flowers, when prices have gone far beyond you, and get just what you want. There

12

will be lovely azaleas for 1s. 6d. and 2s. 6d. instead of 5s. 6d. to 10s. 6d. (which are the shop prices at Christmas-time), Christmas-trees, primulas, and bulbs just in flower. For instance, Darwin tulips with the bulbs just in flower are only 2d. each when they first come in. And everything looks thoroughly fresh and healthy.

In the summer he specialises in rose trees, for he is an expert on them, and people with gardens in the country come to him for advice on the subject. Joe has a shop near the Angel at Islington, and is really quite a well-known horti-culturist, but every day at lunch-time he goes faithfully to Leather Lane and watches "the stall."

"Hi! Hi!—come, come. They're all cheap to-day. Hi! Hi!" Joe's blue eyes twinkle merrily as he calls to his customers. He does not need to shout himself hoarse, but he just keeps up the market tradition by crying out occasionally.

"Hi! Hi!—come, come. Hey! Keep over! Mind what you're doing." Joe's eyes darkened with annoyance, and he looked like murdering the driver of a lorry that swung perilously near his stall of precious plants. Leather Lane is used as a short cut for a good deal of traffic, and the lorries hurtle through as though the market did not exist. There is barely room for them to pass, and they seem to take a delight in frightening the stall-holders and scattering all the people. That is just another of the insults that the proud old lady has to bear, for the motor-cars tear past her carriage, terrifying her poor old horse.

And now come and meet Harry and William Joe. But if you have a feminine heart hold on to it tightly, for like everybody else you may lose it to those two brothers. They are the handsomest couple you can imagine, besides which nobody could help liking them.

They run a fish-stall where you can get excellent fish at very reasonable prices. Everything about their stall is so clean that even the raw fish looks tempting. The brothers themselves are as well turned out as any one. They have fresh,

13

shaven faces, spotless white aprons, and scrupulously clean hands. William, the youngest, has the whitest row of perfect teeth that I have seen and he has a very taking smile.

The Joes are cheery and efficient and very fair to all their customers, while their best recommendation is the number of regular customers, who would not dream of going anywhere else. They number hundreds, and that is in a market where most of the patrons are office-workers who obviously could not keep their fish in the office all afternoon. Housewives come a long distance to go to the Joes' stall, and if you knew them you would not be surprised.

The brothers have a curious history, for Harry Joe, the eldest, used to be an engineer, but when he came back from the War his place had been taken by somebody else. So he started the fish-stall and made an immediate success of it. William was in a printing-works, but grew tired of it, and later on he joined his brother. So began a very happy partnership which brings them far more pleasure than if they had stayed in their highly trained jobs.

"All fish and no bone, makes the baby walk alone," they cried; "sixpence a pound filleted cod. Fresh herrings, little red fish with little red eyes."

"When I was minding the stall this morning," said William, "an old woman came up to me and said, 'A penny bloater and a twopenny pair of kippers—how much, please?'"

"My hat!" laughed Harry; "aren't they bright sometimes? If we have two prices on one kind of fish, sixpence and eightpence, they come up and say, 'What's the difference?' I feel like saying, 'Twopence,' but it doesn't do to annoy 'em."

"There's an old man who shops for his family," William told me, "who always says, 'Give me a piece of fish off the same one as we had last week.'"

"He's a caution," said Harry; "so's the young lady who wanted some fresh haddock and asked me for 'one pound of wet haddock and don't weigh it with the heads on.' I think she must have been newly married or somethin'!"

14

"I had a funny customer before you'd come back from the market, Harry," interrupted William. "I was just unloading a whole lot of herrings on to the board and she came and said, 'How much are you asking for these here?' I said 'Fourpence.' 'Well, pick me out two soft roes,' she says, ' and mind they *are* soft—the hard ones get under me plate in me false teeth.' "

"Oh, I can tell you I had a real time of it with somebody to-day," Harry said. "She asked me to weigh her out a piece of cod, and directly I'd weighed out the amount she wanted, she said, 'No, that's too little, it won't go round.' Then when I put some more on, she said, 'That's too much—he won't eat it.' We were on to that bit of fish for quite a while, with customers lining up and everything."

"Some of 'em spend half-hours at a time running their finger down a bit of cod to see what it's like—course we try and stop 'em doing that. Then there are the ones who always want to weigh their own fish because they think we slap it down on the scales to make the weight go up. One woman has a hunt through our boxes to see if we've got anything better underneath the stall."

"We hear what some of 'em think of their husbands," commented William. " ' Give me a small piece—it's only for the old man.' And some folk always want red spots on their plaice."

"They're quite right about that, Bill," said Harry. "It *is* better fish. But don't they just come and tell us things if the prices go up! 'Fish doesn't cost anything,' they say. Why should it be dear?'"

Most of the stalls close about three o'clock, when the last late-luncher has gone back to the office. But the Joes' stall stays open to the end of the day, for their customers are not the usual Leather Lane patrons and they are busy supplying housewives till nightfall.

One of the stalls with an ever-varying mixed "job lot" for sale belongs to a man called Vincent, who is an ex-waiter

15

from Claridge's; while his confederate, Albert Knie, says he used to be a stoker in the Merchant Service, besides several other things, before he became a stall-holder.

"I've just been to Windsor looking for some job stuff," he said.

It was Mr. Russell, the watch-mender (or watch-maker as all watch-menders like to be called), who told me about some of the street-market technicalities. Tobé men, or "Toby" men as they pronounce it, were the men whose job it was to go round putting up the stalls. But they are practically done away with now, as most of the stall-holders prefer to economise by putting up their own stalls.

"Then what we call 'getting an edge,' " said Mr. Russell, "originates from 'getting a hedge,' meaning getting a hedge of people round you."

He is a likeable person and, apart from watch-mending, he can sell you a very good plain wrist-watch for 2s. 6d.

Tom Kitteridge is known as "The Gutter Poet," "Crying Charlie," and "Weeping Willie," and he sells oddments like beads, razor-blades, and bootlaces. He has a sad, dreamy face, a waxed moustache, and large gesticulating hands. And he nearly always talks in rhymes which he makes up all the time he is standing by his stall.

Hear him selling razor-blades in his own poetic way:

"Well, gentlemen,

"These blades are made of super steel,
  They supersede all others,
If you think I tell a lie,
  Ask the Western Brothers.

(They know.)

"These blades they use in Timbuctoo,
  Newport, and Carolina;
They swear they get the best of shaves,
  And never had a finer.

(A gross for you, sir? Hello! a shipping order.)

16

"What I mean is:

> "I try to convince,
>   I try to make sure;
> Once you try them
>   You'll sure to want more.

"A gentleman asks me if these sécateurs will cut steel. Well, gentlemen,

> "They won't cut steel;
>   They won't cut corns;
> They might cut off a bullock's tail
>   If some one holds its horns.

"Well, gentlemen, I thank you men for your support.

> "For what you buy you won't get caught,
>   It helps to earn an honest crust;
> Without your keep
>   I would soon go bust."

There are some good toy bargains to be got in this market, and father can get toys for his Santa Claus work on Christmas Eve far more cheaply than in the shops. For instance, he can get big dolls, fully dressed, that blink their eyes and speak, for 5s. instead of a guinea, and smaller ones for 2s. 6d. They are carefully packed in a box, so he need not feel ashamed of putting them in the office till he goes home in the evening.

Also there are many kinds of smaller gifts, so plentiful and cheap that schools come to Leather Lane to buy them up in lots for prizes.

Alfred Cross appears each day without a stall and sells one particular thing—but he has something different each day. The day I met him it was paint-boxes full of water-colours—full size paint-boxes with two dozen colours in them, all for 1s. each paint-box.

Leather Lane is open every day always at lunch-time. There is no special day for this market, and it is thoroughly safe and respectable.

17

Some of the stalls are left unguarded for very nearly the whole time they are there—just as though the stall-holders did not expect to sell anything. Other stalls go up, but for some reason there are no wares on them and nobody beside them. They stand looking forlorn and rickety. The rain soaks them through the leaking roofs, and they have no lamp like the others. Perhaps they have no wares because of the rain, and there is no protection when they are tumbling to bits——

I said it was a sad market, didn't I!

Farringdon Street

To anybody who has ever been there, Farringdon Street means a happy hunting-ground crammed with romantic possibilities. It is the book-collectors' paradise. There are stalls groaning under the weight of hundreds of volumes of every sort and kind. Some of them are four and five centuries old, while others only came into being a short while ago. You never know what you may find—and there is always the chance of something really valuable having slipped the dealers' notice, which you can buy for a few shillings to sell again for a fortune or keep among your treasures.

Wednesday is a good day to go, and it is best to be there about eleven or half-past, before the lunch-time crowd. When you come out of Farringdon Station, turn to the right and walk a few yards, when the next turning to the right brings you into the market.

Forget the rest of the market for the moment and go up to the far end of it. You will find you have walked straight into another world. It is a very common phrase that "books give an atmosphere." How true it is you can never guess until you go to Farringdon Street.

There is a kind of silent fellowship among all who go to these bookstalls. Nobody pushes and jostles, or tries to outdo any one. They make way for each other politely, while the stall-holder trusts them implicitly not to spoil his books.

An elderly little man in a mackintosh goes quietly through the books in a careful, assured way. He is a gentleman to his finger-tips and he is probably somebody who has retired to live in a background full of beautiful things and enjoy his hobby of collecting books. Beside him there is an old lady in a blue coat and an old-fashioned hat. She has ancestors anybody would be proud of, but the family money had reached

19

its dregs when it came to her. She has all her wealth in her treasures, and she lives in a world of her own where it does not matter if she has to save threepence on the coal.

A clever-looking professional man has left his work in the office to have one feverish search to see if there are any "finds." And a penniless student is looking for a copy of a particular book for his studies that he can buy for 2d. instead of paying 12s. 6d. for it in a shop.

There is one tragic figure in the group—but even he is happy. An old man, dirty and ill-looking, with unkempt hair and torn, greasy clothing. He cannot buy even a twopenny book because he is starving. Yet he has found happiness in this land of make-believe, while nobody disturbs him or brings him to earth.

The same little group stands there side by side for hours, searching, reading, their eyes appraising all the different qualities of each volume. The rain drips on their shoulders off the canvas roof, soaking them to the skin, but they never notice. Time means nothing to them. It is forgotten. They are all under the same spell—the romance and glamour of old books.

These three stalls at the end of the market are run by George Jeffery. George himself is one of the nicest parts of Farringdon Street, for it would not be the same without him. See his kind, sympathetic eyes as he watches the little group browsing over his books. He just stands quietly near the stalls and does not trouble them. If anybody wants any information he gives it politely and with a wistful little smile. You would never guess the wealth of knowledge and the myriads of interesting facts that are hidden inside his comparatively young head. He can tell you all kinds of obscure details about books, and many other things besides. I doubt if many people with supposedly ten times his education know as much as he does. And he has gained it all from being with his books.

George described to me how he goes to all the book sales and buys the "left-overs" in lots very cheaply. Then dealers

20

and collectors come and buy them from the stalls—and so
the old books go on changing hands until their pages are
fingered completely away.

"One day," he said, "I had a spurious second volume of
Don Quixote, which I sold for 4s. 6d. It was here a week
before I sold it, and apparently a dealer came along and saw
it, but he wasn't sure about it. So he went away and looked
it up. Then he came back and took it. I saw afterwards he
sold it for £100!"

He could have told me many more tales like that, but there
wasn't time. People were buying books every few minutes,
picking them out over the shoulders of the searching group.

Distinguished visitors are an everyday event at George's
stalls—John Burns used to be a regular customer. Jeffery
Farnol and many other authors go to it, while Mr. Garrett
of the British Museum is there quite often. And George is
known and trusted by all the lovers of old books. He will
say at once if anything is incomplete. For instance, there were
five leather-bound volumes of Poe's works which he hastened
to tell me were one volume short. If I had been a collector
I should have bought them at a bargain price on the hope
that a patient search would reveal the missing volume. These
particular volumes had each illustration repeated in three
different ways: one coloured, one in etching, and one on
Japanese vellum.

All the Farringdon Street book-stalls have an astonishing
medley of works heaped carelessly on top of each other. For
instance, on George's stalls I saw Dagenout's *History of Art*
standing beside a lovely old Roman Missal. *Hogarth Moralized*
rubbed shoulders with an illustrated book on poultry.

Apart from the books I saw a whole case of etchings, quite
good ones too, being sold for 6d. each etching. George also
sells people's diaries and the MSS. of lesser-known authors.
Collectors buy both these things in the hope that the diaries
will grow valuable and the authors famous. After all, they
cost so little that it is not an expensive gamble.

Two of George's stalls are filled with miscellaneous old volumes and contain most of the treasures. The third stall has books all the same price, 6d. each, and includes a good deal of quite recent fiction. There are also many legal books on it, and all kinds of educational works.

He told me he has a partner aged eighty. Apparently the partner was "queer" that day, so I did not see anything of him. As far as I could gather he is "queer" most days, but then eighty is too great an age to spend a wintry day in a street market. He is supposed to be an extremely interesting, well-informed old man, and I was very disappointed not to meet him.

The day I saw the book-stall kept by Arthur Acox I could have bought a leather-bound copy of Homer's *Odyssey* for 2d. Arthur has been there fifty years, and he keeps a stall full of twopenny volumes. He regarded me with the deepest suspicion and retired into a shell of completely impenetrable reserve.

"Dutch book—No?" asked a sallow-faced man with a foreign accent.

"No, nothing Dutch," said Arthur, and the man went away.

Farringdon Street is undoubtedly a good place to buy a dictionary. There are dictionaries for many languages, some of them beautifully bound.

"One of the most interesting things," George told me, "is some of the early printing." There are all kinds of rare examples of it among the battered old books in the market, and that is part of their fascination.

Before you know what has happened most of the day has flown by while you looked at the books. But if you can tear yourself away from the spell, there are other things of interest to be seen in this market. If people knock your hat crooked, or upset your parcels when you walk along the pavement, they do not mean you any harm. It is only because they have not come down to earth yet, and they are still completely oblivious of everything round them. They simply have not noticed you. Five minutes ago you were under the same spell yourself, so you cannot blame them.

Miss Petch is a bright-eyed, business-like person who sells old iron and things like rusty old pram-wheels. Her stall is hardly decorative, but some people find it very useful. Scavengers bring up old iron in barrow-loads to the cattle-markets, and Miss Petch is one of the people who buy it from them. Then she makes a shrewd living out of it, among those who cannot afford to stray far from their own locality round Farringdon Street. They may only want one small piece of old iron to make up into something, so they buy it retail from Miss Petch.

Quite a young girl keeps a stall where she sells nothing but flexes for 2d. and 1d. a yard, and she has whole lengths of rubber coils at bargain prices.

Her name is Una Edith Harvey. She wrote it down for me, because she cannot speak. I thought her expression was one of the sweetest I have ever seen. She has a smile that replaces all her words, so beautifully that it does not matter in the least about her not being able to utter them.

"Springs Fitted" is the cryptic announcement on one stall. It means you can have a spring fitted on anything from an alarm clock to a double bed. Or, if you prefer, you can buy the springs and fit them yourself.

People go to Robert Elkington to have keys cut while they wait, for 9d. instead of the usual 2s. 6d. Mortice keys cost 2d. each, and there is an imposing array of locks, padlocks, hasps, and bolts which go at receding prices as the day wears on.

Reginald Clifford carries on a cheery conversation with his customers while he soles their shoes on the spot. Most of the Farringdon Street customers shoe and heel their own shoes. They buy the leather sole already cut out in the shape for 6d. a pair. Then rubber soles are 6d. a pair and rubber heels are cheaper still. Some of the customers bargain with young

23

Clifford over the prices of repair work, while there is a certain amount of good-natured bartering over the rubber heels.

There is a stall where cyclists can get all the "spare parts" of a bicycle. At David Purvis's stall people can get cinematograph machines, camera stands, and astronomical telescopes.

The other end of Farringdon Street Market has a completely different atmosphere. It is devoted entirely to various kinds of food, and there is none of the austerity of the old book-stalls.

I saw one rosy-faced woman, sitting behind a stall piled high with fruit and nuts. As she sat she munched. Her cheeks bulged with titbits and her hand went out automatically to seek a fresh dainty. I wondered how big a hole she made in her supplies by the end of the day, and whether the customers eat as much as she did. But then she was a grand advertisement—she so obviously enjoyed what she was eating.

Strutton Ground

STRUTTON GROUND is supposed to have taken its name from
the way the peers used to strut up and down this road when
they came out of the House of Lords. More probably it is
called after Stourton House belonging to the Lords Desnay,
for it once formed part of the grounds of that house. Then,
when Stourton House was pulled down in 1718, the Strutton
Ground of nowadays became a public gardens called The
Melon Garden or Million Garden, where people went and
listened to the band. Once upon a time the surroundings
used to be a kind of miniature Mayfair. Chadwick Street
nearby is named after Lord Chadwick, who used to live there
in those days.

It is hard to believe that Strutton Ground was once so chic
and fashionable, when there are market stalls along one side
and cabbage leaves on the pavement. Yet only as far back as
1720 the cream of society still used it as their meeting-place.
And the stall-holders are very proud of the fact.

They are also proud of their clients, many of whom are
celebrities of the moment. People can step straight out of a
Rolls Royce to go and do their shopping, without the prices
going up directly they appear. And the market is in a very
handy place for them, because its street is a turning off
Victoria Street, close to the Army and Navy Stores. Before
it came to Strutton Ground it used to be held at the Broadway, St. James's, but that was when St. James's Park Underground Station was still a thing of the future.

I made a special friend in this market. He is tall and jovial,
with charming manners, and a solicitous way with his customers that makes them lay their problems at his feet.

They arrive like ships in a storm, flustered and worried,
their shopping-lists right out of control. He bends down a

25

sympathetic head and unravels the tangled shopping-lists, reminding them of things they have forgotten to tick off, and helping them count their change. The ships have found their calm harbour, and the distraught faces fade into smiles. I thought of him as a Harley Street specialist, or he might have been an eminent psychologist. But he is Mr. James Richardson, who keeps a flower-stall in Strutton Ground.

"I used to box for my regiment during the War," Mr. Richardson told me, rubbing his large strong hands together to keep them warm, "and I did weight-lifting and all that kind of thing. Then I used to play football for the Westminster ———. Of course I never drink or smoke now, you know. I got so used to keeping in training that I've kind of kept in the same ways ever since. During the War I was on the Prince of Wales' staff as his sergeant-major—— Oh, excuse me a minute. . . . Yes, lady. Good-afternoon."

Mr. Richardson turned away to serve a tall, attractive-looking lady customer in a green coat. There followed a quiet, friendly conversation between them, chiefly about flowers, and how long hers had lasted the previous week. Then she picked up her new purchases and took them to a waiting car somewhere round the corner. She smiled to him as she turned away, and he lifted his hat politely as he thanked her for coming.

"That's one of my regular customers. She comes from Dean's Yard, up by Westminster Abbey. We have all kinds of nice people coming here every week. Some of them come long distances from all over the place."

It was then I had a suspicion that Mr. Richardson did some unusual jobs for a street trader. I was right, and I cajoled him into telling me about them, though he was modestly reluctant.

"Well, I did all the flowers for the christening of Lord Esme Gordon-Lennox's baby at the House of Parliament. It was the first christening they'd had there for twenty-seven years, and I expect you remember how there was quite a to-do about it."

26

"The biggest surprise I had was when I was asked to do the flowers for the Robing Room on the State Opening of Parliament. Of course I don't like talking about it, but the Lord Chamberlain sent me a very nice letter afterwards, saying the Queen had been very pleased with what I'd done. I keep that letter as one of my greatest treasures, but I don't like to say much about it," Mr. Richardson added shyly.

We were interrupted by an elderly little woman in a long fur coat. Her eyes roved wildly over the flower-stall, while she tried hard to remember what she wanted to get from it. She was obviously in a state of confusion. Her hair showed signs of coming down altogether, and I think her corns were playing her up after her long day's shopping. Mr. Richardson turned his kindly face in her direction and she hobbled unevenly towards him.

"What can I do, lady?" he asked sympathetically. But the huge effort of concentration had been too much for her, and she stared vacantly at the flowers as though she had forgotten them.

Mr. Richardson waited patiently, smoothing the head of a carnation to avoid embarrassing her. Then she gave a start and there was a sudden gleam in her staring eyes.

"Wreaths," she muttered hurriedly.

Mr. Richardson grew business-like. "Yes, lady. How many?"

"Five," she said hoarsely.

"When you want them by?"

"Monday." At this she brightened considerably. Then there was a kind of earthquake in the fur coat, and she produced an overfilled hand-bag. Letters, hairpins, handkerchiefs, stray curlers—all kinds of things sprang to the surface when she opened it.

It was a terrifying moment while she sought her money, and Mr. Richardson stood with his hands held ready to save the entire cascade of oddments if they should fall. Then, when everything was settled, she thought of looking at her

27

shopping-list. Once more the oddments were liberated and the shopping-list found. But she could not read it. She had been writing on it in the train. Mr. Richardson struggled nobly and managed to read it all out to her. No, she did not need anything else from him that day.

I looked at him after she had gone, but he had not turned a hair. He does that kind of thing several times a day.

"You see, many of them leave things to me. They just come and order their wreaths and things, but they leave it to me how I make them up."

"When do you make them all?" I asked.

"Just here. I put up a couple of boxes to act as a table, and make them up in between serving customers. Then if they have to go by post, I post them that night or whenever they're wanted. Otherwise I have a boy to deliver them for me.

"The late Lord Sankey when he was Lord Chancellor, used to come to me regularly before he moved along. He was such a real nice gentleman. And I have a lot of regular jobs to do all the flowers for various places, like the church opposite, St. Ermins the big hotel over the way, and St. James's Court. Not long ago I did all the flowers for a wedding at Penge. The bridegroom was Liberal M.P. for somewhere in Scotland, and he used to live near these parts and came to me every week."

Then a quiet, capable-looking housewife came to give an approving glance over the flower-stall. She knew just what she wanted and bought her things swiftly.

"Talking of people who come a good way to see me, here is one of them," said Mr. Richardson. "This lady comes from Cricklewood to buy my flowers."

The lady in question looked round and smiled. "Well, it's worth coming all the way when you can get such good flowers and a nice person serving them."

And she did not look like somebody who would have been easily pleased.

"I used to be a supervisor in the Ministry of Pensions since

28

directly after the War," Mr. Richardson continued, "then a few years ago I decided I'd pack up and try this job, and I didn't get the sack or anything. I just hoped I'd do very well at this. Anyhow, it's a good life and it's nice to be one's own guvnor."

At this point he became very busy, so I stayed and looked at his flowers. He had all the early spring flowers that most of the shops had not got yet. And he was not charging prices head over ears for them either. Each separate flower was in perfect condition, and there was no denying they were fresh.

James Richardson will always be my happiest memory of Strutton Ground.

There are very good vegetables in this market. I held a discussion about them with Mrs. Griffiths.

"Me bin here long? I bin here since I was a baby, dear. Me mother used to sit here at this stall with the baby on her lap—that was me."

While she spoke, Mrs. Griffiths was busy peeling sprouts. "People won't look at 'em with the outside leaves, dear."

She is an expert on potatoes, and she told me how to cook them so that they "cook white" in the frosty weather.

"Get some boiling water ready while you're paring 'em, then pop 'em straight into it when it's boiling—draws all the frost out. Some folks put 'em in the water before it boils, and that's just where they goes wrong."

Mrs. Hedges advertised her tomatoes "Like wine—4 for 3d." written in chalk on a brown paper bag. Her oranges had a notice, "Extra full of juice." She said she started there when she was a little girl, with her mother, who had the stall before her.

Her chief joy is her newspaper which she reads avidly between customers and, as she says, she "leaves out nothing."

The salad-stall is well filled even in winter, and it has plenty of good lettuces, though at that time everything is rather superseded by beetroots or celery.

Strutton Ground prices do not compare so well with some

of the other street markets, but they do under-cut the shops. It is probably the smallest of the street markets, and a very nice quiet one if you want to get through your shopping quickly. Friday is one of the best days to go to it, though it is open all the week.

Brixton

LIFE is very jolly in Brixton Street Market. Go down with an empty larder, a large shopping-basket, and a carefree heart, and you will enjoy yourself. But it is a market mainly for housewives, as its wares consist almost entirely of food. The food is fresh, clean, and very good value, while the stall-holders are nearly all cheerful and obliging. They are also highly entertaining.

Thursday is a good day to go, and there are many ways of reaching it. Brixton, to some people, may sound like the back of beyond, but a No. 2 bus that passes through Park Lane and Hyde Park Corner also goes close to the street market.

Most of the stall-holders have nicknames. "Bertie Bacon" is a young man with a spotless white overall, and a neatly arranged stall filled with every possible cut of bacon. He has a great many regular customers, and like the other stalls in Brixton, his opens at 6.30 in the morning.

One woman comes and buys her breakfast there at the same time every morning.

"She's always here soon after 6.30," said Bertie, "to buy her own breakfast. And it's always the same thing she wants, 'One-pound-of-streaky-and-five-sausages.' "

I ventured to remark on her appetite, and Bertie made an expressive gesture with his hands to give me a rough idea of her figure. Apparently even getting up so early in the morning had failed to mitigate the effect of such a breakfast.

"You ought to see her," he said. "It's always the same with 'em—the fat ones are always the ones who ask for the fat bacon."

To give an idea of Bertie's prices: Bacon that is 1s. 6d. a pound in the shops begins the day at 1s. 4d. on the stall.

Green-backs are 1s. a pound. The highest price for streaky is 8d. a pound, when the lowest shop price is usually 10d. and 1s. Towards evening all the bacon grows cheaper, and Bertie takes his stand on a box and auctions the remainder.

Next door to him there is "The Rabbit Man," who sells rabbits, sausages, pork, and turkeys—but mainly rabbits. Personally the sight of raw, skinned rabbits exhibiting a disembowelled stomach to the public gaze is not a sight that tempts me. But the housewifely shoppers studied them unflinchingly.

In the evening, when it is auction time, "The Rabbit Man" has a girl to stand and sell the sausages while he attends to the rabbits and everything else. "Bertie Bacon" has a good-natured grudge against her because she never has any change.

"Eightpence a pound. Half pound? Fourpence. Thank you, lady. Got any change, Bert?" is what goes on all the time she is there.

All day long Bert tells himself that he is not going to be victimised. But when the evening comes he always parts with that change, or even goes round getting it for her. She must have a very charming smile.

I did not spend long at "The Rabbit Man's" stall. It was only those raw, upturned rabbits that drove me away.

And now meet "Fatty," who keeps a bargain-stall of tinned foods. He is one of the "grand guys" of the market, for he has three assistants on ordinary week-days and five on Saturdays when the rush is on. On Sundays his stall goes to Wapping.

You will hear "Fatty" calling out what sounds exactly like "Rotten guarantees!—Rotten guarantees!" But you will soon get to know that he means "Written guarantees," so all is well.

One of the assistants is called Eddy, and he works in a warehouse when he is not on duty at the stall.

"Some of the folks give us a good laugh when they come shopping," he told me. "I was calling out, 'Twopence for two

32

jellies,' the other day, and a woman came up to me and says, 'Haven't you got any penny ones?' She meant it quite seriously, mind you."

Eddy has a great sense of humour and is very tactful with all the finicky housewives.

The chief advantage at "Fatty's" stall is to get a good load of tins of food, in dozens at a time. That way you can get them at very low prices as well as making your visit worth while. For instance, large tins of peas that would be 8½d. each can be got for 5s. 6d. a dozen, which comes to about 5½d. And then there is always the evening auction with "Fatty" in rattling good form.

Albert Coppindale's bananas are only five for 3d. and less. They look delicious, and he keeps them all laid out on clean white paper on the stall. When I saw him it was midday and his supply of bananas had almost gone.

To come down to distressingly feminine details, there is a stall in this market where you can get knickers at a starting price of 1s. a pair. And the starting price in a street market means it will be cheaper later on in the day. These are the artificial silk knickers with elastic that you buy at the draper's for 3s. 11d. and 4s. 11d.

From Mr. Faley you can get excellent fish as good as in any big fishmonger's, and all of it cheaper. Cod is 4d. a pound cheaper than in any shop, while a penny comes off the price of sprats. Whiting is also 1d. a pound cheaper, and herrings 1d. to 2d. a pound less.

You will find he wraps it up carefully in *The South London Press*. But you cannot expect grease-proof paper in a street market, and the reduction is well worth putting up with a little newsprint flavour. After all, you can always wash it off before you begin cooking if you imagine it is there.

At another fish-stall there were some hearty-looking stall-holders calling out, "We do things proper. No rubbish—no rubbish——"

Quite a number of housewives were browsing over the

33

fish there, feeling it with their hands and turning it over to look at the other side. One woman with a very calculating expression was so busy running her finger along a rather distant piece of cod that she knocked down a mackerel with her shopping-basket. Splob! And it hit the pavement with the sound that only wet fish make when it falls from a height. It distracted her from the piece of cod and a horrified expression covered her face.

The stall-holder was on to it like lightning. "Oo never mind, lady. Twopence, please." And before she had time to protest, the mackerel was rescued from the pavement, wrapped up, and put in her arms. She paid for it like a lamb. By the time she began to mutter about not wanting it at all, and it was only an accident anyway, the stall-holder was serving other customers.

In Brixton prices are high for things like cabbages, which are just as cheap in the shops. But for more expensive vegetables, like cauliflowers, there is a very good reduction, for they only cost 2d. each instead of 6d., 8d., and 10d. Tomatoes are 2d. a pound cheaper, and oranges two a penny instead of 1d. each and more. At one stall you can get both floor polish and braces. Sixpenny tins of floor polish cost 3d., while 2s. 6d. braces are only 1s.

There is a good salad-stall which in mid-winter has lettuces, besides mustard and cress, leeks and celery. You can get two heads of crisp celery from a penny. Grape-fruit are a penny each at one stall.

Meat? There is Dick Wright, the butcher, who sells whole legs of Canterbury lamb at 9d. a pound instead of 1s. Shoulders of lamb are 8½d. and 10d. a pound instead of 1s. There is a reduction of 2d. on all joints, compared with the shops. Steaks are as low as 1d. to 2d.

At the end of the day everything is sold off very cheaply. The sale starts at 6.30 in the evening. Dick Wright stands up on a box and holds a quick-fire auction that fills the crowd with excitement. His cries fan the spirit of the bar-

34

gain-hunters and their eyes stare greedily at the joints he holds up. Shall they buy—or shall they wait? There is such excitement. People carry away eight-pound joints for 1s. 6d. to 2s. from that sale.

There is fruit fit for any dinner-party at Alfred Shrew's stall. Mushrooms 1s. a pound when they are 2s. 6d. in the shops, and lovely ripe pears, five for 6d.

"Ataboy! Ataboy!" called "Long Dick," who is as tall as his name suggests. He was selling a game called "hookum" for 3d. when elsewhere it had been sold for 1s. He had a wonderful medley of things that would be useful in a house, but no food.

One person who was doing great trade was a man selling lengths of American oil-cloth for 2d. and 4d. a yard. He was so busy I could not get near him. "I just want a yard and a half—kind a do for the kitchen table," said one ample housewife to another.

"Supposing you've got nothing to eat and you're feeling hungry. It doesn't really matter, because you can easily get a nice large fish. You needn't keep it in the gold-fish bowl or feed it on ants' eggs. There's its eye. The eye's always the same colour whatever kind of fish it is. And there's a very good middle-cut for you to eat. And if the fish smells, you can cut off his nose.

"Now, if you're a burglar, I'll tell you what you can do. Most burglars break a window, and when they break a window they throw a hammer at it. And then they lose the hammer because it's inside. Now, all you have to do is to make a hole—so. Make it just the right size to get your hand through. Then you pop your arm through it, and 'Bob's yer uncle.' "

Just what was all that about? It was Mr. E. M. Edmunds selling a sixpenny glass-cutter. There are no frills about his stall—just the bare boards, and he brings a battered suit-case full of pieces of glass. While he talks he takes out a piece of glass and cuts something out very quickly, like the fish and

35

how to raid a shop-window. His demonstrations are wonderful, and he has an amazingly long repertoire. He is the best entertainment in the market and he deserves to sell millions of glass-cutters.

The Brixton shopping crowd is not a lively one. They are mostly serious-minded housewives with a load of household worries on their minds. Slowly and silently they plod round the stalls, with searching, calculating faces. It struck me they don a kind of you-can't-put-it-over-on-me-because-I-*know* expression directly they set foot inside the market. There is, strangely, little gossip among them, and they are almost terrifyingly efficient over their buying and choosing.

It is the stall-holders who provide the cheery atmosphere. They make the Brixton Street Market—and they make it a gay, delightful shopping centre for anybody who wants to save their money.

North End Road

ONE of London's longest roads runs from Hammersmith to Walham Green. Near Hammersmith the North End Road has modern flats and severe Victorian houses, besides some shops and garages. But the Walham Green end has a street market.

Saturday afternoon is a riot of fun in this market. Like Brixton it is mainly for housewives, but unlike Brixton the shoppers are as gay and giddy as the stall-holders.

Never have I felt the week-end spirit grip me so thoroughly as it did in the North End Road. Hundreds of women had left their cares behind them, and the street echoed with their laughter. They had got through another week, and now they had a fresh supply of housekeeping money. There was all the excitement of meeting their friends out on the same errand, and "the old man" was either at a football match or else out cycling.

They met in groups for gossip, and they bandied with the stall-holders. Prams were pushed recklessly through the crowds, while babies and bargains were compared simultaneously—after all, the prams were used for conveying both. Sometimes a laugh rang out louder than the rest, for somebody here and there had taken a drop of gin.

"Come on, Johnnie, move yerself," said a robust Cockney housewife, hurrying to arrive early at one of her favourite stalls.

Johnnie had barred my path while he stared at me as if I was an apparition. His liquorice lay suspended on his tongue, while his mouth hung open with astonishment. He had detected a stranger and he wished to investigate me. But a lusty arm tugged him away and he was forced to yield to superior strength. Poor Johnnie, he was beginning to lag

37

already, and I had been a welcome excuse for resting those little short fat legs.

Anybody who has forgotten their shopping-basket goes straight to Rubins Morris, who sells large, roomy shopping-bags for 6d. each. Most of them look rather like a patchwork quilt, but they are very well made. He makes them himself out of any stray bits of leather or American oil-cloth that he can find. In the North End Road he just stands on the pavement with his shopping-bags heaped at his feet, but at the Caledonian Market he has quite a big stall. "Carrier bags—sixpence each—carrier bags—only sixpence, lady."

I went over to a big fruit-stall covered with tempting things. But I could not look at it because of two women customers. One was a huge, jovial person, with a bright red face and eyes that rolled expressively as she talked. Her companion was a smaller woman with a lean face and hair that hung in stiff grey twigs beneath her hat. They were rollicking, and they had come to tell the stall-holders everything they could think of.

"You did ought to 'ave seen 'er on New Year's night in 'er beaded dress," said the jovial one; "didn't 'alf fancy 'erself."

And the smaller woman bared a fence of wide-apart teeth. She giggled with delight.

"I like yer basket, dearie; aren't you going to put somethin' in it?" said a stall-holder, hoping to remind her of the fruit-stall.

"Why, all the shopping she ever did in her life was to buy that there basket," said the jovial lady, with louder giggles.

But the little woman waved the empty basket in her face, just to show her independence. "I bought a turkey for 'alf a crown and carried it home in this," she bragged. "I'm going now to look for its mate." And she turned away to go down the market.

The jovial one followed her, screaming, "Ta, love, ta, ta," to the fruit-stall woman.

38

But they did not get very far. I found them a few yards farther on, heads close together, deep in some new titbit, with the market entirely forgotten. I doubt if they did any shopping that afternoon.

"I say, girls! I say, girls!" cried a butcher inappropriately, as two old women passed him in the crowd. His stall was surrounded with a bevy of women armed with forks, prodding busily, and searching for a tender piece. In some of the other street markets they go up to the meat and pinch it. But in the North End Road they are given forks. And they prod.

Later in the evening the meat that has failed to pass the fork-test of hundreds of housewives is sold in a gay, quick auction. Perhaps this treatment has made it as tender as the rest. Let us hope so anyway.

"Penny a bunch, Ma!" said a vegetable-seller waving a bunch of parsley at a harassed woman pulling a pram. There were two children in the pram, and a great many parcels which they were investigating with rather more destruction than care.

One of the children had already made his way into a pound of granulated sugar. He was taking it out in handfuls and eating with relish. His brother was banging his feet on a basket of eggs. But their parent did not seem to notice—she was far too engrossed in her shopping.

"Pork and veal, girls! Pork and veal!" This butcher sold good fat roasting chickens for 1s. 6d. Near him was a man selling blackboards, complete with an easel, for 4d.

"I walked in in me blue—lookin' me best, and he was fair took up with me straight away. Went to the pictures two nights runnin' with him I did. The old man didn't 'alf 'ave a fit . . ."

A group of three women had collected for gossip. They stood and scandalised each other with huge enjoyment, amid shrieks of laughter.

"I 'ide all the 'ousekeeping money in a box underneath

39

the gas-stove, dearie, otherwise it's gorn once he gets a fist on it for a drop a drink."

" 'Ave yer seen Gertie's new 'at? Looks like a flower-garden after a storm . . ."

The group grew larger as more acquaintances tacked themselves on to glean what they could. There were continual greetings and more stories. But, unlike the first two, these women had done most of their shopping. They planted their heavy baskets on the ground at their feet, and settled down to their gossip as though nothing else mattered.

Mrs. Alf Cheyney does good trade with her sweets, on account of all the children who come to this market. Early in the morning and late at night she is busy making sweets on her own kitchen fire. Then all day she sits behind the stall in the market, with her rosy face and white overall, looking the cheery, kind-hearted soul she is. The children all love her, and very few parents have the heart to drag them by. And her sweets are cheap, with many variations.

One woman with a fruit-stall was dusting her wares vigorously with an old feather broom. After the dusting she sprayed them with a disinfectant syringe. I wondered whether she was merely giving them a wash, or whether some people's fruit would be served smelling subtly of disinfectant.

Mrs. Priddle, wearing a white apron and long ear-rings, sold her fruit. She had lovely dessert pears for 1d. each, when the shops were charging 3d. to 6d. each.

"Potatoes, try 'em, real good," was written over Mr. Reading's stall. And they looked good too, and were cheaper than elsewhere.

"Pick out any sort you like," called a man selling heads of celery.

Then I met Mrs. Hodgkins, the "grannie" of North End Road. She has been there longer than any one—about forty-two years—and now she sits on a stool all the time to save her dear old legs. Most of the shoppers stop and have a word

40

with her, and the stall-holders seek her cheerful philosophy when "things are bad."

Her stall is a vegetable one in winter, and in the summer she sells salad greens. There she sits, in all weathers, chuckling and smiling at everybody, with her wrinkled face and round, rosy, turned-up nose, and such twinkling eyes. Life has ceased to trouble her. She has learned how futile it is to worry. "They come and they go, but mostly they go," she said gaily, when I asked about her customers. And she probably says the same about all her worries.

As I left I turned round to look at her again, and she gave me the broadest wink I have ever seen. I shall always have a very tender memory for Mrs. Hodgkins.

"You didn't ought to buy from 'im, 'e isn't up to no good," advised one housewife to another. But then it gives a kind of spice to the shopping if you can only throw a little suspicion here and there.

On a Saturday the North End Road Market is lined with small boys holding out a head of celery or a bunch of bananas —calling out in high piping voices, and trying to inveigle people into buying them. They are mostly children of the stall-holders endeavouring to earn a little pocket-money on their own account. The idea is for them to catch the people who are walking past and not going to stop at the stall. Some of them make themselves very useful.

Just by the winkle-man's stall I ran into Mrs. Sirkett, who is a very ardent shopper in this market. She was quite spontaneous about making friends with me, for friendships are formed easily and quickly in the North End Road. Women meet on a common ground there and a very favourite one— shopping.

She was a small woman with a sweet, good-natured expression, and she had a small son who she grasped by the hand while she was talking. I could not see him very well, as he was evidently addicted to tearing off his hat and flinging it away. It was put on so firmly that it hid half his face.

41

"Oh yes," she told me, "I always do all my shopping down here. Do it all in two days a week, I do. I have to make it two days because I get me groceries one day and they're a lot to carry home. Titus Wards is my grocer and a wonderful grocer he is too. I'll tell you for why. They give you a shilling in the pound, and you don't have to sign a book, and there's nothing to pay. Yer just take yer slip each time, and then end of the month or whenever you want you take 'em all along and collect the rebates. Give over, dear; leave things alone."

The rapid flow of information was cut short by her off-spring, who was attempting to get at the winkles.

" 'Course I live up by Olympia," she hastened to assure me, "but the shops have such high prices there and not always fresh either. It's worth coming down here, really it is. 'Ullo, Mrs. Griggs!"

A friend passed and nodded to her and was lost in the crowd.

" 'Course I come and do me shopping here of an afternoon before the crush comes. Bein' a regular customer they treat me kind and let me 'ave things reasonable. But if you want to do some bargaining you should come in the evening. Though the crowd's so thick by nine o'clock you can't move."

It was then I interrupted by thanking her gratefully, and she went off to finish her complete round of the market.

My big moment was when I met the merriest trio of stall-holders in the North End Road—Mrs. Botley, Mrs. Frost, and Mrs. Kerrins.

Mrs. Botley was sitting by a stall filled with all kinds of household oddments, like soapflakes, floor polish, and scrubbing powder—all going at cut prices. A sixpenny packet of soapflakes begins the day at $5\frac{1}{2}$d.

"I've bin here thirty-four years," she told me, "mindin' this stall for me Dad. I'm a bit late to-day because I've had a drink—well, it's the truth. Went for me drink at one-thirty, I did, and didn't get back till three-thirty. Well, it's the truth; why not have it, I say."

Mrs. Botley's husband is a taxi-washer, and when she had told me this she introduced me to Mrs. Frost, who had a fruit-stall next door.

"You ought 'a meet Mrs. Frost, she's got ten kids."

"Thirteen, I used to 'ave," corrected Mrs. Frost after this startling introduction. "I lost three, I'm sorry to say."

Lemons are two a penny at Mrs. Frost's stall at a time when the shops are charging 1½d. and 2d. each.

"People come and ask me if the lemons are sweet sometimes," she said with a high laugh.

"Whoy! Whoy!" A small boy passed us, waving a solitary sprat. In his other hand he had an enormous biscuit-tin presumably for conveying it home.

Mrs. Frost introduced Mrs. Kerrins, who sold vegetables at the next stall and was even more lively than the other two.

"You ought 'a 'ear what some of 'em say, dearie," she said, when I was asking after her customers: " 'Ha'penny worth of watercresses for the dicky-bird,' or 'Penny beet-root and are they well done?' Then it's 'Give me a small piece of parsley just for the dish.' "

She recounted all this to me amid many gurgles of laughter, and in between each story she seized me by the arm. I was very sorry when I had to tear myself away, but it would have been unkind to stay, she had so many customers.

There was a stall of household goods that had a kettle boiling away on a little stove. "Nellie's lung syrup—Free" was painted on the kettle. I was told it meant the stall-holder gave away free cups of tea to her customers. Then, while their inner man was being warmed, she would interest them in her goods.

"Nellie" in this case was away just then, so I could not try her "lung syrup." She must be a clever person and I should like to have met her.

Just then there was a fearful commotion the other side of the street, and the shoppers swarmed to see what was happening.

43

An old woman selling pea-nuts was standing calling out her wares close to a man selling bootlaces—rather too close apparently, for the next thing was he had words to say about her shouting him down. She retaliated by giving him a piece of her mind, and she went closer to him to do it. Then he pushed her. It was quite a gentle push, not meant to knock her over but only to intimate that he resented her screaming angrily into his face. Yet, very strangely, it overbalanced her, and she sank all too easily into a sitting posture on the pavement while the pea-nuts rolled everywhere.

Then she began screeching at the top of her voice, invoking the help of everybody, including the police. And the police did arrive just then, but they showed no more sympathy towards her than they did to the bootlace man. They seemed to have a shrewd idea as to what had really happened.

Meanwhile, the bootlace man was busy telling the crowd exactly what he thought of the pea-nut woman. Of course it made an excellent opportunity to advertise his bootlaces.

That was only one of the little interludes that happen in a street market. It was a very short one, for the police quelled it in no time, and the crowd dispersed sheepishly to continue their shopping.

The food is very reasonable in the North End Road and reasonably good. And the serving is exceedingly quick and obligingly done. I have yet to find a shop that comes up to it in this way.

Those who want to get through their shopping swiftly and unimpeded should do it in good time on Saturday afternoon. But if they want the real next-to-nothing prices they must face the crowds in the evening and bargain with the rest.

44

Choumert Road

THERE was a gale blowing when I went to Choumert Road, one of the worst this country has known. Lives were lost at sea, and scaffolding killed people in the streets as it was torn from half-finished buildings. Imagine the agonised time the stall-holders had, with their little old wooden stalls that the wind picked up like matchwood. They were trying to hold them to the ground, and at the same time prevent hundreds of goods from taking flight in the teeth of the hurricane.

This is a courageous little street market, holding its own against the famous covered market which is only in the next turning off Rye Lane. Little-known Choumert Road really deserves an important place beside Farringdon Street and Leather Lane. It has some of the best bargains and the most interesting people you will come across. I have a sneaking fondness for it that cannot be crushed, even by the glories of Caledonian Road.

"A. Smith" has a stall that spells adventure. Anybody looking at it for the first time might sum it up in one word, "junk"—but they would be making a bitter mistake. Accept the invitation to "Please walk in," and you may make some startling discoveries.

When I was there it was presided over by a quiet, sleepy-eyed young man called Sydney Cosbolt. Like the stall, his appearance is deceptive. He looks as though he had nothing to say for himself, yet when he does talk to you he is a mine of interesting information besides being kind and obliging.

He showed me a newish white three-piece bedroom suite for 35s., and a whole suite in satin walnut for £4, 19s. 6d. You could get a washstand for 3s. 6d., complete with the china. A big solid leather trunk cost 3s. 6d. too. It was rather like the stout old ancestral trunk that is brought down from the attic in Noel Coward's *Family Album*. And the words, "There it sits—frowning at us," came back as I looked at it, wondering about its history. It was certainly frowning in the street market. I felt it was like a very old man being mocked by small boys, and I almost bought it out of pity for its degradation.

There were old-fashioned mahogany escritoires for 1s. 6d. each. Nobody makes them nowadays, and they might be worth buying, as they will probably become a valuable curio in another generation's time.

"Last week I sold a sixteenth-century sampler," said young Cosbolt; "about the year 1700 its date was, and I suppose somebody went and made a fortune out of it."

He was shy about giving information at first, but when he grew more confident in me he produced his prize of the moment—a lovely little Sheraton clock, which he was prepared to let go for 50s. The works had dropped to bits and almost vanished long ago, but the little wooden case, so beautifully made, was still in perfect condition. I expect by now it will have found its way to Christie's or else gone to a collector to whom it is far too precious to sell.

"We often get dealers asking us to look out for certain things they want. Then, when perhaps they turn up months or even years later, we have to let them know."

Just as he was speaking, a boisterous gust of wind knocked down a 35s.-set of huge pieces of china, splintering it to atoms on the pavement. Sydney Cosbolt bore it without a murmur, but it must have been a heart-rending blow to him. He just picked up a broom and swept away the pieces. Evidently he was a fatalist as well as an expert on old furniture.

"We've had some excitin' times with old settees," he continued, while our ears still sang from the crash of the broken china.

"How?" I asked.

"People used to hide money in 'em—also things sometimes drop out of folk's pockets and go down into the settee,

46

so that they never know where they've gone. We've often found money tucked down inside, and one of the first things we do when we get an old settee is to look and see what we can find. The other day a friend of mine, who works with old furniture too, found a hundred and thirty-six pounds in gold sovereigns tucked into a fusty old sofa."

James Warner sells all kinds of bulbs and roots 4d. cheaper than the shops, and lily bulbs are 4d. each instead of 9d. That is during the day. In the evening he sells up everything in an auction, when things go cheaper still.

I found Mrs. Robinson having a systematic spring-clean of her entire haberdashery stall. She does that all day to pass the time in between customers, a section at a time, and the whole array is beautifully neat and clean. She sells everything that "haberdashery" covers, like cotton-reels, elastic, combs, safety-pins, and suspenders—only in her case there are a few stray bottles of aspirin and cascara as well.

The kind of combs you can buy for 6d. are 1d. and 2d. each, while medium width elastic costs 2d. for three yards. There are "cottons and silkos, two for $2\frac{1}{2}$d." Apparently she buys them all up in big lots from warehouses when they become disused stock, which does not mean they are unusable for the public.

"Saturday night's the best night for this market," she told me, "but Friday's very slack here. Thank you very much—much obliged," she added to a customer as she sold her some yards of elastic.

"Noted for English wild rabbits," is how Charles Turner likes to be introduced, and I think I can safely say it, for he is very honest. They cost 7d. to 1s. each, or you can buy them cut up, ready for cooking, for 7d. a pound. He also sells pickled pork to go with it for 9d. a pound, which is 3d. a pound cheaper than the most reasonable shops.

Mr. Turner has a nice life, for he buys the rabbits from farms all round London, even as far afield as Sevenoaks and Tunbridge. He goes over the farms himself on Sundays and

Mondays, discussing the prospects in the rabbit world and keeping up a friendly personal contact with the farmers.

People buy dog-fish in the Choumert Road. "Eightpence a pound and very nice eatin'," said Mrs. Welch, who minds the stall, "and there's cat-fish we sell too, that's just as good and same price, eightpence a pound. Has a head on it exactly like a cat."

Mrs. Welch has other varieties of fish, too, like haddocks and fresh herrings, but cat-fish and dog-fish are very popular in Camberwell.

"Me and my son does the stall between us," she told me; "me son drives the van while I stay here. Quite welcome, dear." And she nodded farewell to me, for the fish was going well that morning.

"Got yer veal? Got yer birds? What would yer like, lidy?" asked Albert Coombes.

"Everything starts a penny a pound cheaper than the usual price," he replied to my inquiries. "I have an auction on Saturday night, when I stand up on a box and sell by weight. We can't sell anything under the hammer here. If we sell by hammer we're liable to get locked up. But if we sell by weight we only get locked up for obstruction."

There is a queer substitution for a lending library in the Choumert Road, and you will find stalls like it in some of the other street markets.

William Hammond presides over a stall full of magazines of the "penny dreadful" type. People buy sixpenny magazines for 1½d. each. Then, when they have read them they can bring them back and change them for different ones, free of charge. Also, those who bring him half a dozen magazines for his stall get about three or four in exchange. And so they go the round until they are worn to nothing.

Nobody minds about the date of the magazines. They only date back to any month last year or the year before. It is all

48

a case of whether they have read them or not. That is all that matters.

"Ha'penny comic, please," said a little girl whose head only just came above the top of the stall.

"There you are, missy, help yerself."

She had brought back another comic, so she did not have to pay anything, and she looked through the pile of comics with an air of importance while she sought out one she had not read. Children's comics are cheaper than the magazines, and so are little boys' adventure numbers.

Mr. Hammond has a cheerful rosy face and a very kind heart. His mouth was so full of bread and cheese when I discovered him that I found him a little difficult to understand. And as he was chuckling merrily as well as eating and talking, that made it harder still.

With such a gale blowing, the entire contents of his stall might have vanished to the other end of London. But of all the stall-holders he was the most thoroughly prepared for it. His magazines were all held down by a row of pieces of string fixed tightly across from one side of his stall to the other. This way it was impossible for the wind even to flap their pages, let alone blow them away.

There were titles like *The Unknown Wife* and *Her Only Sin*. A spinsterish woman in glasses was looking through them with bright, greedy little eyes. She was rather troublesome because she had read nearly everything that was there. Mr. Hammond had to delve inside his reserve stock in a box underneath the stall before something could be found that would satisfy her, and she gave a little squeak of delight when it appeared. Then she popped the new number into her basket—a story crudely saturated with passionate indiscretions, in which she could soak herself to her heart's content.

I had a long conversation with Mr. E. W. Bird, who is the "Pussie's Butcher" of Choumert Road. He sells horseflesh for 7d. a pound as cat and dog meat, and condition powders for both cats and dogs. I saw some embrocation with a

49

picture of a horse on the bottle, and asked if he tended horses as well.

"No, the embrocation's for human bein's," he said; "the horse serves to cheat the medicine-tax and they just call it 'white oils.' Here's a horse's liver, and this is half a horse's tongue. This here's a horse's heart—cats love 'em all."

Mr. Hammond came for some change just then, and Mr. Bird let him help himself.

"Put that down," said Mr. Hammond, playfully ducking his head, for the cats'-meat man was still flourishing the horse's heart.

"I get the horse-flesh already boiled from the horse slaughterers," Mr. Bird continued; "boiled by steam it is."

He has been in Choumert Road "nineteen years come next September," and he is devoted to his four-legged customers.

"One dog comes and sits on 'is 'ind legs in front of the stall and won't go away till I give him three pieces. If I give him two and pretend that's goin' to be all, he still waits till I give him three. Some of the dogs come to me and wait here till their owners come back from their shoppin'."

Mr. Bird does many kind things for people who cannot afford a vet.

"If animals are queer, I go home and see 'em for them," he said.

He has just one pet of his own.

"I only got one cat. There's more children in my 'ouse than anything else. My son's upstairs and he's got four, the youngest three months and the eldest six. And there's me own two small kids, one's twelve and the other's six.

"On a Sunday there are eighteen in my kitchen. My son brings 'is family from upstairs and my daughter brings 'ers in. Every Sunday, and the same time, when it's hardly past seven in the evening.

"Eight adults and ten children, and there's not ten minutes goes by when there isn't one crying. One'll tread on another's feet, and then grandmother'll pick one up and another one

50

starts hollerin'. Talk about a monkey-'ouse, it isn't in it. I just sit in me chair and let 'em get on with it."

Mr. Bird's stall looks rather like a Punch and Judy show —so quaint and high up, to be out of the way of canine marauders. Framed inside is the smiling face of the excellent little showman himself.

Berwick Market

YOU have to be very strong-minded to visit Berwick Market. The stall-holders press you much more than in any of the other street markets, and some of them make it an embarrassment for you not to buy anything. This applies especially to the stalls that sell clothing, and going through them at a slack time is rather like being sucked into the mouth of an octopus. Rows of brown eyes try and hypnotise you into buying something, and when you pass by you can feel them darken behind you.

But this is nothing to worry about—especially if you want a good pair of stockings. Nowhere else can you get such lovely stockings for bargain prices. But, as in all the street markets, you have to buy carefully and with an expert eye.

One of the best stalls to buy them from is a stall belonging to a woman called "Fay." There you can get thin, pure silk stockings for 1s. 3d., and fully fashioned ones for 2s. They are beautifully sheer and fine. "Fay" is not too pressing with her wares. She is just quietly kind and helpful.

Even women who are dressed by Hartnell and Schiaparelli have owned to buying their stockings in Berwick Market. It is quite a common thing for very chic people to be seen there, while chorus-girls from all the theatres find their Mecca in the Berwick stocking-stalls.

Having made sure of the stockings, it is an advantage to buy a great many pairs on one visit, because then you can bargain with confidence and be sure of a good reception another time.

Just after the War, Berwick Market did excellent trade, but nowadays it is very quiet.

"If the rain keeps away, we're all right," commented "Fay." "I bin here since I was ten years old, when I used to serve in the evenings after school. And the stall still keeps in the family."

"Business used to be so heavy that they had to close the market on a Sunday," said Micky Migdol, who sells materials. "Now they could close it three times a week and they wouldn't miss anybody."

"My materials are fifty per cent. cheaper than the shops," he continued (that may be so if you can bargain well), "and people come here and buy materials, and then leave us to dye them how they want."

"There was a film taken here not long ago, called 'Mr. Cohen takes a Walk,' all about a man who started by having a stall in the market. Then he rose to be head of a big drapery store and a millionaire, but he came back to the market and had a look round, because he had so little to do. Still, that's by the way. Some of my customers spend nearly all day here, wanting to see every piece of material and asking questions about it. Then in the end they go back to the piece they saw first."

"Good afternoon. This is very fascinating, if you only knew," called a woman selling nightgowns.

Madame Max sells "slip-and-knicker-in-a-box, 3s. 6d." She does good trade with them on Saturday, when perhaps the price descends discreetly for a regular customer.

Gloves from Mrs. Gordon cost 2s. 11d. instead of 3s. 11d., and if you get her in the right mood they may cost less. She has been there twenty-two years.

Most of us are tremendously keen on buying remnants for making odd bits of lingerie, or even little silk jumpers for a tailor-made. It is nice to know of somewhere where one can get them at times between the remnant sales in the shops. And this is where I must introduce Harry Coleman, who has a stall full of attractive remnants all the year round, costing an average price of 6d. to 1s. a yard for the best silks and woollens.

Dresses that would cost about 35s. to £2, cost 17s. 11d.

54

each, and sometimes it is worth while to get one for everyday use and have it altered elsewhere. There is very little fitting done in the street, as you can imagine. The frock is just laid up against the customer, and then everybody hopes for the best.

Mrs. Kerners is a nice, friendly person to buy frocks from, and she is another one who was bred and born in the market.

"We 'ave a very 'ard life in winter, but it's very nice in summer," she said. "We start at nine-thirty in the morning. Business begins about two o'clock—if any," she added sceptically.

"Oxford Street has knocked out Berwick Market," she continued, with a sad look in its direction.

This stall serves customers for orders for things made to measure. They have a staff of a dozen girls sewing for them in a building nearby. But there is something which makes them feel infinitely more important—electric lights in the street market. Mrs. Kerners showed me how they had plugs in the wall by the pavement, from which they attached a flex and electric bulbs to light the stalls. The other street markets have oil-lamps, which need constant trimming and polishing to woo them into giving any light at all.

Conversations are often amusing in Berwick Market.

"I can't put me 'ands down 'em because me nails are jagged," said a house-worn woman who was buying some stockings.

"They're orl right, dear, really they are—not a flaw in 'em anywhere."

"Orl right, I'll believe yer." But the customer's voice was reluctant.

"Yer can believe me," triumphed the stall-holder. And the stockings were bought.

"Pull yer in, duck, pull yer right in slim," called the woman with the corset-stall. An enormous shopper, carrying about seventeen stone, gave her a look that might have killed. Perhaps she knew too well that stays alone could not alter her dimensions. Possibly she had tried in the past, and her resentment was all the keener.

It is Madame Birnberg, who has the corset-stall, and it is well worth a visit. Dainty satin suspender belts with rose-buds on them, that usually cost 5s. 11d. to 7s. 11d., are only 1s. 11d. there. And you can get every sort of garment for what advertisers call "figure control" at equally low prices. Further, you can take things home, try them on, and bring them back and change them if they fail to fit. The sizes go from the slimmest petite up to a forty-inch waist and fifty-six-inch hips.

"They all like to be pulled in," Madame assured me. Evidently her own special street-cry usually strikes home.

Mrs. Cohen sells quite attractive hand-bags for 5s. each, and she also has a stocking-stall across the road. Somehow or other she manages to keep her eye on both of them. Also customers who buy hand-bags are taken over to see the stockings, and the reverse thing happens to stocking customers.

A blonde young beauty holds court at a cut-price perfumery. Her name is Gertrude, and the stall is called by the grand name of Bromhill's Stores. Threepence comes off 2s. 6d. jars of face-creams and other things, and 6d. off the 4s. 6d. preparations. And Gertrude is nice-mannered and obliging.

If you pass by without looking at his beads and bags, Mr. J. Smith says, "Yes, Madam, don't mind serving you!" to remind you he is there.

"How much is fivepence and twopence-three?" asked a customer, fumbling with her change. She was so flustered she couldn't for the life of her do such a problem of arithmetic.

People who enter the market by Little Poulteney Street have to go through an arcade of dress-shops to find the main part of the market. Bold-eyed "girls" of the district stand in the doorways—watching, waiting—trying to draw customers into the shops. Their make-up is crude in daylight, and they have black crimped hair, shiny with brilliantine.

56

Those who go through the arcade a second time, on the way back from that part of the market, are subjected to a certain amount of insolence. The girls fire remarks to each other as you pass that are scarcely complimentary.

"No, I've sorted her inside out, already." "She ain't up to much, anyway." "Doesn't look as though she knows what a dress means." "Too 'igh 'at, dear, anyway." "I'd sooner put a dress on a scarecrow as put it on 'er."

That is just their charming little revenge on you for not visiting their shops when you went by before.

Berwick Market straggles into several of Soho's streets, including Little Poulteney Street and Rupert Street.

In Rupert Street there is Soloman's antique shop, which is patronised by a great many important celebrities. The people are honest enough there, and it is a wonderful place for picking up interesting things.

I saw a letter from a very influential customer in the United States, and English well-knowns are in there almost every day. The shop has been going for fifty years, and it comes into this street market, as it has a street stall of three-penny books, some of which have realised £40 when sold again by collectors.

I saw a set of four hundred-year-old celery vases going for £5, 5s. (or less to some people). There was an old Georgian cake-basket, a crucifix from Rheims Cathedral, old candelabras, and some china made in 1886.

People came in and bought dozens of knives and dozen sets of table silver, for prices far below an ordinary silversmith. They had good glass there too—lovely old table glass of all kinds. One day, when I have a fortune, I shall go and spend some of it there.

D. E. Smith was the assistant who showed me round, though he was too busy to devote too much time to any one person. You can go in there and look round for as long as you like, without being pestered to buy anything. Mr. Smith is very quiet and nice-mannered. He told me they often work on commission for customers, going round to all the sales and buying things for them. But they only do that for private customers and not for dealers, though they serve a great many dealers in the shop. Between them the assistants can speak French, German, and Dutch. They need it, too, with all the foreign visitors they get. Soloman's is quite a favourite spot for collectors from all over the world.

In Little Poulteney Street you will find a stall with the words, "Jack Smith—The B.B.C. Broadcasting Fruiterer," painted on its board. Here is another person who has broadcast in "In Town To-night." When I went to see him, Jack was not there, and two lively young assistants were keeping the stall for him.

One of the assistants was Jack's own son. "Father served King Edward with pears," he said, " and he's served the King and Queen of Spain with all kinds of fruit. Lord Ashfield was one of his customers and Lady Bland-Sutton. That was during the War when food was so scarce, and we served Lord Ashfield right up till last year, when he went away. Forty-two South Street he lives at. And there's Stanley Baldwin's niece we serve too."

The other assistant told me something about the less celebrated customers who see a thick-skinned orange and say, "Oh, that's been boiled." This is a housewifely rumour about thick-skinned oranges which has no truth in it.

"One customer came and squeezed a coco-nut to see if it was ripe."

Then the son suggested he should take me to meet his famous father, who was away reviving himself at a coffee-shop—"quite a respectable one," he assured me as we started off to find him.

There we found plump, jovial Jack, sitting on a high stool having his afternoon cup of coffee and bit of gossip.

"I was the first man to sell tomatoes in the streets of London," he told me. "They were originally imported from Spain fifty-six years ago. And now I sell all kinds of queer fruits, like shaddocks, that are twice as big as a grape-fruit, with a pink inside. I sell pomaloes too. They're smaller than a grape-fruit and white inside. There's monsteria as well, that looks like a cucumber, and custard apples, mangoes, passion fruit, læchees, and avacado pears."

Incidentally his avacado pears are much cheaper, and just as good, as the ones you buy in a shop that specialises in rare and costly foods.

He told me some well-known people he was serving at the moment, including Lord Hartley, who lives at the Kensington Palace. He also serves the German and Persian Embassies.

"I was the first man to sell grape-fruit in England, about forty-six years ago. You know it's a cross between a shaddock and a pomaloe, and it was first grafted in Jamaica. Would you like to hear how I came by them?"

Would I not!

"Well, the first hundred cases were in Middlesex Wharf, Wapping, and they came up for sale on Monday, Wednesday, and Friday, and nobody would buy them. Then, later on, there were a whole lot more came, and they were all up for sale again in Pudding Lane, which was where they sold the fruit before Spitalfield. I put me finger up. And I got five hundred cases for a shilling a case, and there were eighty grape-fruits in each case. That meant I made two hundred and fifty pounds' profit out of it."

There is nothing Jack does not know about grape-fruit, and he is probably the greatest expert on it in the country. He told me the best grape-fruit comes from British Honduras.

He invited me to stay and have a cup of coffee with him, and I wished I could. But the afternoon had waned and, unknowingly, I had tramped many miles round the stalls. There is so much to see in a street market.

New Cut and Lower Marsh

NEW CUT—

THIS is an unpleasant chapter. New Cut is an unsavoury market, though for those who attend it I suppose it must have many redeeming merits. It is just another phase of the street markets. You might dip into it once to complete the adventure and that is all.

Waterloo Station brings a vision of comfortable long-distance trains, holidays, Southampton, and luxury liners to America. But if you were to go behind its back doors you would be going down the grim pavements of the Waterloo Road. New Cut is a turning off this road, and it runs from the Old Vic to The Ring. The stalls straggle all the way down one side—not a long distance if you measure it in yards, but there are few things to shorten it in New Cut.

The last stall by The Ring was a tiny little ramshackle stall filled with dusty tins of boot-polish, stray pairs of boot-laces, and a few stale pieces of soap grown white and crumbling at the edges.

A young woman stood behind it with a pram and a baby each side of her. Her face was deathly pale under its coating of grime, and her eyes stared hopelessly out of hollow cheeks. They may have been her own babies, or perhaps they were borrowed to draw pity. But they probably were her own, because who could fancy for a minute that pity could be found in that district. They sat up in their prams and sucked their tiny cold fingers as though they were never going to take them out of their mouths. The dribble had chapped their faces and made runnels in the dirt. They were as pale as their mother, and she did not rock their prams or try to

61

cheer them up, for she was beyond it. She just stood staring in front of her—waiting for the customers who did not come.

A fish-stall reeked so horribly that my footsteps slewed away from it as I passed. There were three pieces of dog-fish laid on the boards—nothing else. So it was they alone that accounted for the atmosphere surrounding them. A man was dusting them with a dirty old oil-stained rag. Dust has a way of clinging to the food in New Cut, and most of the stall-holders give up trying to remove it.

On a banana-stall many of the bananas were half opened. This was done to show people how good they would be to eat, but instead they were merely assimilating dirt, while the skins grew untemptingly brown at the edges. The same thing happened at the orange-stalls, and the half-skinned oranges looked as though they had been serving as the stall's advertisement for the past fortnight.

One man sold second-hand window-boxes and knife machines piled up on top of each other. Some of them lay in the gutter. China cups were 1d. each, without any saucers —nobody wants a saucer anyway.

People can buy goats' milk and live eels, and they can get home-made wines "by the glass." Cordials, like strawberry, clover, or blackberry wine, cost 1d. to 2d. a glass. They pour a little into the bottom of the glass and fill it up with water, as it is an extract. This is quite a popular plan, for there are several men selling it. One of them has no stall, but takes his drinks round in a home-made hand-cart. This vehicle makes such a noise with its wheels that it cannot fail to attract attention of some kind, though not always of the right sort.

I found one advantage in New Cut, for you could get three keys cut for 1s. 9d., and there was a candle-man whose candles looked fresh and clean and were going very cheaply.

An old woman in a man's cap and an old sealskin coat was sitting by her vegetable-stall, where she had a lighted brazier

62

for baking potatoes. She was eating a baked potato, gouging it out of its skin with a knife and gobbling it off the end of the blade, while she talked hard with her mouth full. She was so dirty she looked just as if she had come straight out of a coal-mine, and her vegetables shared the same appearance. Half her sprouts were tumbling on the ground, and potatoes were crushing the leaves of her cabbages.

Most of the women wore men's caps, but there were very few amazons beneath them. They were far too starved.

Opposite the stalls the houses are blackened and decayed, their windows silted up with grime and their doors closed unwelcomingly, with filth thick in every crevice. There is a forbidding atmosphere in this street, as if it threatens you not to find out too much. I heard afterwards that there is a great deal of crime in it.

The street market is scarcely a happier part of it. Existence there is just a gaunt grey skeleton. Prices are ridiculously high on the labels, though it is obvious that no one takes them for granted, and the wares are grimy and untempting. The stall-holders seem almost to resent the appearance of a stranger. When I asked one man his name, his eyes rolled to and fro, while he tried to make one up. He was shifty, evasive, and suspicious, and he obviously had something to hide.

I did not linger in New Cut, but fled away home, trying to forget the haunted eyes of the woman with the two prams.

—AND LOWER MARSH

On the opposite side of the Waterloo Road, exactly opposite New Cut, is the Lower Marsh, where there is a street market only a little less depressing than its neighbour. At any rate it has more life in it, and many more wares. And somehow it seems far less sinister.

There is a large pea-nut-stall where you can buy a big bag of them for 1d. Cooking dates at another stall are only 2d. a pound before bargain time.

Some of the stalls are queer ones—like the one that has old books, old boots, and pram wheels. The atmosphere here is clouded, not so much by the fish-stalls as by the old clothes, which also include cast-off pillows and old mattresses.

I saw two boys crouched in a telephone-booth for a smoke and talk in the warmth. Farther on, two women stall-holders, with buckets of water on the pavement, were busily washing tins of metal-polish to make them look new. At a stall near-by you could buy a four-foot bath for 6s. 11d. or less, and a full-size dustbin for 3s. 11d. A man selling cough-drops was the most enterprising person. He had quite a fair crowd round him, while he gave a long peroration in a strangely ecclesiastical voice.

"Give you a big twopennorth, for a cough, for a cold, bronchitis, catarrh—and remember they will cure your cough, gentlemen. I wouldn't pass them by, they're value. . . ."

While he was speaking the cough-drops were being brewed at the stall, sending out a strong smell in the process.

I was startled by loud shrieks, and two of the Lower Marsh belles emerged from a doorway, arguing at the tops of their voices. Then they set to and fought like demons, laying on to each other with their fists, even using their teeth and putting in some good hard kicks.

In a moment the dejected, loafing crowd was galvanised into action—not to stop the fight. Here was something they liked, and a fight between two women was even more exciting.

I did not see the end of it, for it did not appeal to me to the same extent, but I heard them shouting at each other when I was half-way down the street.

New Cut and Lower Marsh

It is said that on a Saturday, New Cut and Lower Marsh follow the tradition of all street markets and hold big auctions that draw thick crowds. Perhaps for those few hours a shade of happiness steps into the hearts of the New Cut shoppers.

Lewisham

THEY call him "Mad Ginger" in Lewisham Street Market. He is twenty-six, ginger-haired, and he comes from Somerset. His nickname is no reflection on his wits, but is meant as an approval of his wit which has made him a famous young character in Lewisham. Ginger's real name is Frank Alford.

"You ought to meet Mad Ginger. 'Ee's the one in this market. 'Ee goes quite mad sometimes of a Saturday night," said a stall-holder who is known as "Mush." And so I went to look for him.

I had to wait about for a long time on a freezing cold day. When I got to his stall he had gone to Catford, on an errand for a young vegetable-seller called Mary Sales.

"He'll be back any minute now," said Mary Sales encouragingly. She is a sweet little person with a smiling face, and she sells all her vegetables for a little cheaper than the shops.

"I used to be a cook in a public-house," she told me. "Then I started helping my husband on the stall, and when he died I took on."

When I went back for the third time she called out, "'Ere 'e is," and she nodded smilingly towards a horse and cart that was driving up the road. "Hi! Ginger! There's a lady wants to speak to you."

"Na! Not to me," said Ginger impishly, but he pulled up his horse and cart beside us.

"I can't stop and talk now. I'm busy; I've got to put Kit into the stable," he added, pointing to the horse. "It's cold, and she's been out since five this morning."

But I pleaded, Mary Sales pleaded—and he suggested I should go and have a cup of coffee with him. He led Kit into a little alley-way nearby, where he covered her with all the stray pieces of sackcloth he could find in his cart, and we went into a coffee-shop in the alley.

It was a very small coffee-shop, kept by a quiet, reserved, middle-aged man, who made me think of churchwardens in country churches. He ought to have been one instead of keeping an alley coffee-shop—but he made lovely coffee, and he obviously had a good influence on his customers.

We took two stools at a little table by the counter, and there was one big table in the corner as well where people came and ate lunches. I had a Lancashire lad sitting beside me, who joined in the conversation and helped things out whenever Ginger had a spasm of shyness. There were two young men at the big table who joined in too sometimes. And a very small boy, eating a large plate of steak-and-kidney pudding, who said nothing at all. Once I tried to be kind and said, "You're having a fine meal, aren't you?" But he only gave me a deprecating glance over the top of a clouded pair of spectacles and went on eating faster than ever.

While the coffee was being made, Ginger told me how he came to Lewisham.

"I lived in Somerset till I was nine. Me father was a farmer. Then me mother married again and came to London with me stepfather. Me mother was a Londoner, so she wanted to come back, and me stepfather was a basket-maker and wanted to come here for better trade. Then I went to school in Woolwich and when I left I went to work as a bottlewasher. Fourteen I was. After that, I think I was fifteen or sixteen when I went to a brewery, bottlewashing at Lovibond's. Then to the fruit game here."

"Tell 'er some of yer wisecracks, Ginger," suggested the Lancashire lad.

But Ginger was shy. "Most of 'em aren't fit," he said. It was probably only too true, for street-market humour is often distinctly broad—especially on Saturday night. However, he did come out with a few of his more presentable ones when he was half-way through his cup of coffee.

68

"Peas and no maggots. . . . Brussels free from the fly—Mrs. Russell, come an' eat yer nobby brussel. . . . Mrs. Baker, step this way for yer old tater. . . . Rhubarb recommended by all quack doctors and better than any pills. Split tomatoes, five pounds a penny—fetch yer basins."

"Why the basins?" I asked, and he explained that there is a sale of split tomatoes on Saturday night. Paper bags are useless for them because they go soft and break. The Lewisham housewives know this, so they collect the spoil in basins to be on the safe side.

These are only a very few of Ginger's wisecracks. He has many more of them, and he draws the biggest crowd in Lewisham every Saturday night. When he is not at the stall he goes errands, and does "cartage work" for the other stallholders with his horse and cart. Sometimes on a holiday he takes them for a joy-ride instead. He bought Kit in Deptford for £15.

"Somebody asked me for 'a pennyworth of carrots, parsnips, turnips mixed, an' sprouts as well, and not too many sprouts.'" Ginger chuckled reminiscently, and pushed his hat further over the back of his head.

I tried to draw one of the two young men into the conversation, but he only smiled nervously from his corner.

"'Ee's the banana man," said the Lancashire lad, who was less shy than anybody. "'North, South, East, or West, Sam's bananas are the best!' That's 'is cry."

At that point "Alice" popped her head in at the door to see what was going on. She is Alice Hillyard and claims to be the oldest street-trader in Lewisham (I should hate her to know it, but some one else claimed precisely the same thing). There have been three generations of street-traders in her family, and she is very proud of it.

"It's the gipsies what came and spoilt everythin' here," she interrupted. "The gipsies from Farnborough. We had to turn them out of Salisbury Yard for all the dirt of 'em."

69

"Why Salisbury Yard?" I asked, rather bemused, and hoping there were no ex-gipsies in the coffee-shop.

"That's where I live, dear. They come and ruined the street-tradin' in these parts. Still, I'm not afraid to speak the truth. That's why the magistrates rely on me. When I stand up in the police-court they know they'll get the truth out of me. That's what they like to 'ave."

I failed to see how magistrates and gipsies had anything to do with my conversation with Ginger, but as it had been interrupted I said good-bye to my coffee-shop friends and went back into the market. Before I went I left the church-warden-like shopkeeper a sixpence, but he would not take it, so I bought some cigarettes with it instead and handed them round. There are endless West End waiters who might well be supplanted by the coffee-shop man. He simply did not know the meaning of an itching palm.

And now there is "Mush"—another light of Lewisham. "Mush" specialises in mushrooms, though he sells fruit as well, and he is really Mr. Herbert Thomas Reeves.

"Fresh every day," he calls; "morning gathered. Every day we 'ave 'em. Guarantee you'll come back for more. Look at mine an' other people's."

Let me recommend them. He is the first fruiterer I have met who sells every sort of mushroom and knows for which purpose each kind is best. And they are all perfect specimens, besides being reasonable. They average 1s. a pound when shops sell them for as much as 2s. 6d. to 4s. 6d. a pound. Best white buttons are good for stewing he will tell you, open mushrooms for frying, and then he goes into all kinds of knowledgeable details about them.

Most of them come from the Chislehurst Caves in Kent, where there is a large mushroom industry that began not more than two or three years ago.

"Mush" has been street-trading since he was fourteen years old. Another good line he has are big Bromley cooking apples, which you can buy cut up as "cut-up apple, 1d. a

70

pound." "I'm the only chap who's ever done it," he told me, swelling out his chest beneath a woollen waistcoat that had one button missing. It was kept done up by a piece of bright yellow wool. You would like "Mush." He is a likeable person and he knows a very great deal about mushrooms.

Harry Jeal has apples for 2d. and 3d. a pound, and tangerines are four a penny. Large grape-fruits are only 2½d. each in this street market. Most of the fruit is cheap and good, and there are lovely flowers. Mr. E. Wadsworth sells "saucepan scourers a penny each, and greaseproof paper a penny a packet."

Mr. J. Less has a very good show of flowers. To give an idea of his prices, narcissus are only 3d. a bunch, while they are 10d. a bunch in the shops. His wife helps him by making all the wreaths and crosses.

There is a luscious salad-stall kept by kindly Mrs. Davies, who sells endives for 6d. each and less, instead of 8d. Big crisp lettuces are 3d. each in midwinter.

"I have plenty of customers who live on salads only," she said. "They diet on it for different complaints—certain diabeteses" (she said it like that) "and all that. Salad's especially good for it."

You can easily find Lewisham Street Market, as it is on one side of the High Street, near a fare stage that is called "The Obelisk or Clock Tower." It is one of the freshest-looking street markets and very gay-spirited as well. Monday is a dull day, but from Tuesday onwards the market life grows more and more brisk and vivid, ending in a frenzied climax of high spirits and quick selling on Saturday night.

The first stall in the market, nearest the Obelisk, is a very useful one to all who possess their own kitchen. He is the Herb-man, Charles Walker, and he sells every kind of herb that is used for cooking and seasoning.

There is parsley, two kinds of thyme, rosemary, bay-leaves, sage, marjoram, tarragon, garlic, and even bottled horse-radish, besides many others. All the herbs are 1d. a bunch, and

71

Charlie never cries his wares, though he probably holds a silent bargain sale on a Saturday night.

One of the young wits of Lewisham is a young man called "Fred," and he does a tango on the pavement with a young woman stall-holder next door called "Lil." Fred cannot resist a bit of fun at any time.

One day he saw a very prim-looking old lady walking down past the street market with an expression as though she was going through a miniature Hades. This was too much for Fred's sense of humour, and he rolled in front of her, pretending to be drunk.

She fled in terror into the local Woolworth's, whither Fred pursued her, rolling and hiccupping. First she hid behind one counter and then another, but he always followed her. In the end she hurried out into the street again, and took to her legs with far less dignity than she arrived. That was where Fred returned calmly to his stall, wiping his hands and winking soberly at "Lil," who was reduced to a state of abandoned hysterical laughter.

Lewisham street market is lots of fun and certainly an excellent shopping centre.

Lavender Hill

IT was her curls that struck me. There were so many of them, and they were so incredibly neat. I only saw the back of her head at first, because she was busy serving fruit—a tiny figure perched on high heels and wearing a white overall.

Then I went up closer, and I saw all those curls were even kept inside a net so that the wind did not ruffle them. There was a jaunty little brown hat on top, pinned to the curls with safety-pins.

I waited for her to turn round. Would she be pretty, or would she be . . . ? I could hardly bear it. I did so hope she would be pretty—and she was.

Louisa Kelly had the sweetest little face, with wide blue eyes, a clear skin, and a happy smile.

"My brother and I run the stall for me father," she said. "Sydney's in the shed just now, where we keep the stores, but he'll be out in a minute. He and I 'ave been minding this stall for eleven years between us, ever since Mother died. I was the only girl amongst five brothers, and now the other brothers are all gone to work, but I still run the house for father and the family. Then there's a little boy we've kind of adopted, because he's got no mother and father and his sisters go out to work."

There was such a flow of customers that she had to stop and attend to them. I watched her flitting from one to the other, quick and practical the whole time, and always obliging. There were tangerines, three a penny, canary bananas two a penny, delicious grapes 5d. a pound, big cooked beet-roots a penny each.

Presently she turned to me with another smile, and I could not resist admiring her curls. But it was all right, she was pleased, and evidently quite accustomed to receiving com-

73

ments on them. She patted them as if to see they were still perfectly in place.

"Oh, they takes me about two hours at least to do every night—eighty curls there are. I haven't been to a hairdresser for nearly two years."

A woman came round to the back of the stall after she had done her shopping and asked how much lemons cost. Then she whispered something in Louisa's ear and Louisa popped one in her basket on the quiet.

The customers still came pouring in, so our conversation had to be very disjointed.

"How'd it be if I went and called Sydney?" she suggested, and she went running a few yards up the street, called out to him before she went back to the shoppers.

Sydney was very like Louisa—good-looking, blue-eyed, and friendly. He was twenty-two and the youngest of those five brothers, while Louisa herself was only twenty-four.

"Look what I've just had," he said, handing me a folded piece of paper that he took out of his pocket. It was an order from one of his customers:

"DARLING SYDNEY,—

> 3 lb. apples to cook,
> 1 lb. tomatoes,
> ½ doz. peaches,
> head celery."

"We often get a string of children lining up to see them across the road," he told me.

"And do you do it?"

"Yes—only too pleased." And I knew he meant it.

"We 'ave a salad-barrel as well just beside the stall on Fridays and Saturdays. We were the only people selling fresh apricots for sevenpence a pound yesterday, when they'd got none in the shops. Nobody else had plums round here in January; we had them, fivepence a pound, from South Africa.

74

"You ought to see me when it's raining sleet an' hail in a high wind, sitting on top holding a sheet down to save it goin' up in the air, an' Louie holdin' on to the other corner."

We were interrupted by a woman shopper who came up to Sydney just then. "I'll 'ave you up fer breach of promise," she said, with a twinkling side-glance at me. "You a married man an' all."

"What do you want?" asked Sydney, laughing.

"A wooden box. I 'aven't a bit of fire in the 'ouse, and the old man's moaning like I don't know what."

Sydney dragged out an empty vegetable-box and gave it to her with a good-natured smile. She thanked him warmly and carried it away with her. As she got to the end of the street she turned round and called out, "It's a thousand pounds I'll be wanting."

She was a wonderful person, amazingly active, with a pale, wrinkled face that had astonishingly bright twinkling eyes. Probably she had a pretty dreary time with her "moaning" husband and sadly inadequate supply of housekeeping money. Yet she was a bundle of humour, and she obviously had a bizarre sense of fun over all kinds of drab things.

Then I heard more about Sydney's and Louisa's brothers.

"There are two with stalls of their own at Balham," said Sydney. "One has veg. and the other fruit. Then one's a motor-driver and the other does engineering work. Of course Louie and I stayed to keep this stall going, because father has to be away doing all the buying. It's been here twenty years and it does good business.

"It was our mother who started it and really got it going like this. Before that, she had one at Clapham Junction."

As he spoke of his mother, Sydney's face grew radiant.

"She was wonderful, she was one of the best. Do you know, we've got so many of the old customers she had before she died eleven years ago. And there was one woman who'd gone away to live in the country just before me mother died, and she came back nine years later and asked how she was

75

and why wasn't she here. That kind of thing's always happening. They never seem to forget her. She was so good to everybody, and she always used to take the children across the road. That's why we go on doing it ourselves, Louie and I."

Wednesday morning is quite a good time for Lavender Hill, where there is brisk shopping and plenty of noise and bustle. Like most of the other street markets it is gayest and busiest on Saturday afternoon and evening.

You must not expect a street with about fifty or sixty stalls along it. Lavender Hill is a wide main road of Clapham, with fast-moving traffic, and shops down each side of it. The stalls are dotted about in twos and threes in odd side-streets. Men and women stand about selling strips of elastic or paper flowers, mint or buttons. They have no stalls, but they cry out lustily, and as there is so much noise already they have to shout very loud to outdo other people. A walk up Lavender Hill is quite amusing because of them, but the stalls are mainly vegetable-stalls and not really very engrossing.

It was Louisa and Sydney Kelly who made Lavender Hill for me.

76

Rye Lane

Only five years ago Rye Lane was a real street market, and a very famous one. Then it was moved into a special concrete yard, called Market Parade, where it is partly covered in. But it has kept its old fame as a street market.

This, it is said, will eventually become the fate of all the street markets. They will gradually be cleared from the streets and pushed into special arcades. It will be a sad day when that happens, for they are such a vivid part of London's character. But improvements often bring tears when they take things away.

A notice caught my eye and made me stop:

"TO-DAY'S BARGENS—

Belly Pork (with spots on), 6½d. lb.
Frying Stake, 6d. and 8d.
Best Livir, 8d.
Pork Chops, ½d. each."

This was not a display of illiteracy, but was done on purpose to amuse customers who came to D. Gorston's butcher-stall.

Many of the street-cries are distinctly crude in their type of humour, but the butchers' cries are usually the crudest of all. That is why Willie Howes, who is very good doing his bit on a Saturday night, had to think very hard before he could tell me any that could be put into print.

They will take up a stout leg of mutton, give it a resounding slap, and say, "There's a leg like my young woman's leg."

"Small joint of beef put up for a lady with one husband," cries Willie. "A large joint of beef for a lady with a small husband and a large family. Breasts of mutton a penny each. We don't sell 'em by weight, we sell 'em by the yard. Wash well, keep their colour, and if you wash 'em in Lux they won't shrink."

Apparently Willie had just sent up a true story about one of his customers to an evening paper that was running prize contributions of Cockney humour.

"It was on a Saturday night," he said, " and there were about forty people standin' close in front of me, when a small lad came and pushed his way through to where I was standin'. He was so dirty that I asked him, 'What yer bin doing, mate? Playin' with water?' 'No, I haven't.' 'Well,' I says, 'what d'you want, mate?' 'I want three-pennorth of steak.' So I asked him, 'What d'you want it for? Eatin' or cookin'?' And he gave me a witherin' look. 'No,' he says, 'I want three-pennorth steak for two hungry men and they *don't* like a lot of fat.'"

"Another day I had a kid come along and say, 'I want three-pennorth of scrag, please, and make it as much as you can—we've got seventeen in our family.'

"We always serve the kiddies well. It's the guvnor's rule. He thinks that when they go home they might get into trouble if we don't give them a bit extra, and perhaps the parents tell them to go somewhere else."

The butchers' store where Willie works has another stall in Lewisham Market. I thought Willie was the nicest person in Rye Lane.

Another person I liked was "Jack," who does the cries for a big fruit-stall called Manzi. He has a comical face, merry blue eyes, and is usually friendly and amusing.

"Lily-white parsnips," he cries, pointing to some that are smothered with earth, "carrot and turnip and onions, make you broth like brandy. Taters, sprouts, cabbage, these are the best. Broccoli all the rage from Broccoli Jack."

Mrs. Brown sells five good oranges for 2d. at her fruit-stall, and six-pound family cabbages are sometimes sold for about 4d. or less.

The mystery man of Rye Lane is one who sells new and

78

second-hand shoes, and styles himself "Moses." Nothing in the world will make him divulge his real name, but his history is astonishing. He has been a chef in a restaurant, a soldier, a sailor, and a shoemaker. Besides all this, he has seen many vicissitudes of hotel life, having been in the business in all kinds of capacities from porter to second-in-charge. And now he is a very lonely figure standing beside his boots and shoes, with a little stall in an open part of the yard, waiting for people to buy shoes or bring him repair work. He does all the repair work at home after he leaves the stall, and his new shoes cost anything up to 6s. 11d. and the second-hand up to 4s. 6d.

His advertisement was also one of the crazy-spelling variety. He had a board stuck on a lamp-post with "Don't be shody shod" chalked on it.

"Moses" is only a young man, and I hope his luck will turn again one day, because he does not seem very happy among his shoes.

Opposite "Moses" there is a nothing-over-twopence stall, kept by a man called Rosenberg. You can get an amazing variety of things there for a penny or twopence. Soaps, toilet-rolls, hair-nets, exercise-books, combs, cold cream, and vanishing cream are only a few of them. When I saw him he was most proud of some white elephants with upturned trunks. They were very beautifully made, but I did wish he would not tell me they were alabaster.

There is an enormous display of coats and frocks in Rye Lane for prices well under £1. And there used to be a miniature fun fair inside a red striped tent, but when I saw it, it had been stopped by the police. The tent itself remained hopefully on, but for the time being it was deserted.

This market probably comes second to Berwick Market for coats and dresses, and the display is always well in keeping with the season.

The place where the old Rye Lane Street Market used to be has now become a big amusement fair.

79

Battersea

MRS. HALL is a very charming Battersea housewife, with four children and a husband to keep as well and happy as she looks herself. And she does all her shopping in Battersea Street Market.

I discovered her after I had already had some highly embarrassing interviews with other Battersea housewives, who were far less friendly than she was.

It was the empty shopping-bag that made me accost the first one. She turned a heavy-jowled face on me, and gave me a look as if I had just broken into her house. "Wha?" she said fiercely. I repeated my wish to accompany her on her shopping expedition. "Wha?" she said again, more fiercely than before. Then she evidently decided I must be a lunatic, and in a more humouring tone she said, "Na! I'm not going to do none to-day," and turning a massive back on me she began shopping immediately.

The next woman was kind, but she was very old and very deaf, and everything I said had to be repeated by her small grandson who piped lustily into her ear. "Never mind," I said, with a smile at both of them.

I tried another woman. She was worse than any of them, because she gave me one startled stare and took to her heels as fast as she could, looking back furtively over her shoulder every minute to see if I had gone.

And then there was Mrs. Hall. "Why, yes," she said brightly, "certainly, if you like. I'm not doing much shopping to-day, but you can come along with me if you want." So I thanked her and fell in beside her.

Our first port of call was a big butcher's stall at a corner where there was a noisy auction going on. We joined the crowd of watching, waiting women, and fastened our eyes

81

on the meat. Every one was silent and intent. I was fascin-
ated by a grim old woman who stood at the front of the
crowd with her lower jaw stuck out, her eyes roaming
greedily over the joints that passed through the auctioneer's
hands.

The young man who held the auction said his piece exactly like a machine, and he looked as though he was bored
stiff with the whole thing. There was a large blood-stained
sheet behind him, hiding the place where the carcases were
cut into joints, but if one peeped round the side of it there
was a really unappetising view of the whole process.

Mrs. Hall, I noticed, did not watch the auctioneer. She
was busy giving each piece of meat that hung on the sides of
the stall a minute examination, even to the most distant ones
right at the back. The auction did not appear to interest her
in the least.

Perhaps she guessed I was wondering over this.

"You see that joint he's got there," she said, nodding at
a big piece of meat that was being held up just then. "See,
it's all frozen. You can see the ice on it. If you were to take
that home and cook it, you'd find it would sink in the middle
and shrink away. And you'd have far less meat than you
thought you would."

"Here's a fine shoulder, anybody. One-an'-two. One-an'-
two, anybody," called the auctioneer. "One shilling, anybody. Anybody, one shilling. Well, I don't know. Somebody seems to be in a hurry," he finished sarcastically, as
the crowd stared in solid silence and he had to throw it down
and try something else.

The next piece of meat shone juicily. "That's not frozen,
is it?" I asked Mrs. Hall.

"No," she said, "that's not frozen," and I saw by her face
she would tell me more later.

"Anybody want to borrow a couple of quid to see 'em
over?" called the auctioneer as he handled the piece of meat.
"Now come on, everybody. One-an'-two. One up the

middle there." And he flung the joint to a girl assistant to be wrapped up for a bidder.

When he was just going to take up a fresh joint, Mrs. Hall pointed to a leg of lamb hanging far up in the background. "I'll see that," she said quietly. He took it down and weighed it. "Five pounds—two-and-four." "Thank you, I'll have that." And she paid for it and took it.

It had looked such a dried-up joint that I had wondered at her taking it. But she volunteered an explanation.

"You see, those bits of meat that he held up looking so fresh had been wet with water to make them look like that. If you take a dried-up-looking bit, you can know it'll cook up nice and cut tender, because they haven't kept it long enough to have to do anything to it yet."

Most of the street market in Battersea High Street is devoted to food, but at the far end, near the railway-bridge, there are several junk-stalls and stalls selling old clothes.

When we left the butcher, Mrs. Hall stopped at the first junk-stall at the corner.

"Mr. Collins, I see you've got a jug and basin there," she called pleasantly to the man behind it.

"Yes, lady, I have," he said politely.

"How much is it?"

"One-and-sixpence and quite all right, lady." He turned it over for her to inspect.

"Yes, I'll take that," she said.

"Right, lady; I'll send it."

"Have you got a small table big enough for two people to eat off?" she asked next. He had one, but she did not like it.

"Maybe to-morrow," he said consolingly.

Then we passed on. I noticed Mrs. Hall had not paid him, but counted on him to deliver the jug and basin at her house. They seemed to know each other well.

"You see, if you get to know these people you can trust them to send things or keep them for you, and they'll be quite honest with you. I've been going to Mr. Collins for a very long time now. Yesterday I got a wash-stand from him for a shilling. My sister's starting up a guest-house, and I'm helping her find bits of furniture for it."

There was a cut-price grocer shop on the inside of the pavement, where Mrs. Hall filled her basket with a whole collection of things like soaps, sugar, and cheeses. She was extraordinarily quick and efficient over her shopping. I could see she never dawdled or stopped to gossip.

"I come down here every day and do my shopping," she told me. "It's just as good any day in the week in this market. And it's worth coming, because you can save about threepence on each thing and you can always know things are cheaper than what they are in the shops round here.

"My boy comes and gets the vegetables and fruit for me in the morning, and any of the odds and ends. But the meat and fish and that would be too difficult for a child, so I have to choose those myself. Then the flowers my husband gets here when he comes through the market on his way from work."

She showed me the flower-stall, and I saw they were selling big bunches of lovely mimosa for 2d. each, when the shops were selling them for 1s. 6d. a bunch.

"I don't pick any particular stall for fruit or veg., or fish either," Mrs. Hall remarked. "Gardner's fruit is very good."

Our little shopping trip was finished all too soon. But Mrs. Hall's basket was full and her arms were aching.

"I'm sorry I can't stay any longer," she apologised, "but you know what it is when you've got all the work of the house to do."

And she gave me a cheerful smile and hurried home to her family.

84

Hammersmith

"THE second turning on the right, up King Street," said the policeman at Hammersmith Broadway.

This street market is tucked away in a little side-street of its own, and entirely fills it up, for there are stalls on both sides of the narrow road. There is a friendly, happy-family atmosphere about it, both among the stall-holders and the shoppers. It is also one of the few street markets that are worth visiting on a Monday. But it does not get busy till lunch-time that day, probably because Monday is wash-day for the Hammersmith housewives. Saturday night the stall-holders are full of jokes and original cries, but they do not call out much any other time.

Mrs. Butterfield was the first friend I made in Hammersmith Market. Her face radiates her kind heart and robust good health. She has been selling fruit at that stall for twenty years. While she was talking to me she was very busy going over the apples and oranges with an old feather broom.

"What gets me down," she said laughingly, "is when customers ask me for 'a ha'penny lemon in a bag, or a pennorth of grapes in a bag.' They can't understand the bag costs me nearly as much and be content with a piece of paper."

A man passed us carrying a bunch of long strips of elastic. "Silk elastic," he called in a high, wheezy voice. He is to be seen at most of the street markets at some time or other.

"I sometimes get people who come and takes an orange or something off the front of the stall," continued Mrs. Butterfield, "and that upsets the whole lot. *Then* I 'ave a good few words to say.—'Ullo, dearie, you come to see me again," she crooned suddenly, as a small child in a pram appeared with its mother.

85

After that an old man wandered over from his onion-stall across the road, beaming and stroking his stomach.

"Feel better now, love?" inquired Mrs. Butterfield.

"Aye," said the man, sucking his teeth reminiscently.

"Yes, so do I. Just 'ad me dinner, duck," Mrs. Butterfield chuckled.

Then she took me to see Mr. E. Dear, who has a fish-stall. I waited while he picked up a little girl and sat her on his shoulder. She had come to do the shopping on her own.

"Where are you goin' and what do you want to buy? A pennyworth of whiting? You shall have it," he said, putting her down again.

When she had gone, Mrs. Butterfield introduced me to him and he gave me a good-natured greeting. His stall has been through three generations, for it was his grandfather who started it. He said street-cries were not necessary with stalls of long standing, and that is why they have almost died out in Hammersmith except for Saturday night.

Dear's fish is 2d. a pound cheaper than in the shops, and he always has a wide choice of all the seasonable kinds of fish.

"Most of the customers have been going to me all their lives," he said. "I knew 'em all when they were children."

Just then Mrs. Butterfield came rollicking down the pavement again. "Just you be careful and remember I'm watching you!" she called out archly.

"There now," chided Mr. Dear, "I was just going to take her to the pictures this evening."

"Well, take my advice and sit in the front," she advised playfully; "if you sit at the back every one'll see you as they come in." And she capered off to attend to another customer.

Mr. Dear suggested I should talk to a rosy-cheeked young man who kept a rabbit-stall not far down the pavement, and took me down to meet him. While I was talking to him I learnt that he was James Dear, a son of the fish-stall man.

James Dear was skinning rabbits with astonishing rapidity the whole time he was talking to me. He told me he began

86

skinning them at eight o'clock and went on all day, only stopping to attend to customers. I asked him what happened to the skins, and he said, "We sell 'em to a firm that cures 'em and makes fur coats and bowler hats from 'em. English rabbit skins fetch more than the imported ones.

The Dears are a very industrious family, and their two stalls probably carry the heaviest business in Hammersmith Street Market.

"I go to market at four-thirty in the morning these days," James told me. "Me mother usually goes to market and buys for the two stalls, but she's got blood-pressure just now, so I do it. Then I've got another brother, you know. He drives a lorry and runs a garage, and his bit for the stall is hanging all the skins up to dry. Then me sister she sells at my rabbit-stall, and there's another sister apprenticed to a florist, and me married sister she comes up too and helps on a Saturday. Then I've got a crippled sister, but she stays at home, and it's a bit dull for her, with all of us out to work."

This was as much of the family history as I had time to hear. James Dear sells very good sausages, while his rabbits are to be well recommended.

Hammersmith is altogether a food market, with cut-price household goods as well. Mrs. Butterfield said there was a flower-woman down at the King Street end who is very amusing, but I missed her the day I was there.

I saw the cheapest cooked beetroots in the market, for they were three for 2d. and a good size at that.

"Two a penny, two a penny," called a little boy, holding out a bunch of bananas. "Two a penny," he cried insistently, thrusting them in front of each person who went by. "Two a penny—two a penny—all the bloody lot for twopence," he finished up angrily.

You must never be shocked in a street market.

Shepherd's Bush

STALL-HOLDERS crying their wares, motor-cars and prams pushing through the crowds, babies yelling, people gossiping, things being loaded and unloaded, trains going by on the embankment, dogs barking and birds twittering, and above all the music of dozens of cut-price gramophone records.

These are only a few of the sounds that signify the Shepherd's Bush Street Market. They all join together in one tremendous joyous din that echoes loudly through the alley all day long.

The alley is brimming over with stalls so that they almost bulge out of it at either end. You will find it just by the railway-bridge off the Shepherd's Bush Road, and the railway runs alongside on the high embankment. Saturday morning is the best time to go, because by the afternoon it is almost impossible to move for the crowds. Even by midday nobody can walk very quickly. And when a van comes through to deposit provisions, the crowd billows out into the stalls, dragging prams and shopping-baskets out of the way as quickly as they can.

"What you see you get, you know, girls," called a man selling meat. He was interrupted by a little girl who wandered along with her eyes glued to the ground, sobbing bitterly.

"I've lost my key," she muttered tearfully, as he held out a sympathetic hand.

"What sort a key is it, duck?" he asked kindly. But she was so distraught she could not even describe it.

The best place in London to buy nuts is at William Poulteney's stall in Shepherd's Bush Market. He supplies people from all over the town, and even has customers who live miles away in the country.

89

"Walnuts are always the most popular," he said. They are 7d. a pound at his stall, and you can get all the other usual kinds of nuts there too. His are not the kind of nuts where you have to say a prayer before you crack each one.

"I sold three ton of nuts at Christmas alone. Twenty-four sacks in those four days. And I always have to keep eight sacks each side of me, besides having the stall crowded. I bin here sixteen years by the way."

You cannot miss Mr. Poulteney's stall, because it always has such an amazing quantity of nuts on it.

Films are developed for 3d. in Shepherd's Bush, and matches are only 6½d. for a packet of a dozen.

"Any conger eel?" inquired a woman at Mrs. Johnson's fish-stall; " 'ee don't like fillets."

"Yes, I know what yer mean—you'll 'ave to get them somewhere else though."

And the woman went off to see the Eel Man.

I found the Eel Man myself, but it was not my happiest moment. His name was Mr. Cooke, and he had a row of basins full of wriggling live eels in front of him. I noticed a gory-looking board covered with equally sanguine fragments of eels, and in a voice weak with nausea I asked if he slew them on the spot.

"Yes," he said, wielding a long knife dripping with blood, "I'm the murderer. I ought to be round the corner at the Gaumont-British studios." And he winked at his own grisly joke.

Apparently people buy live eels there for 1s. a pound and, when Mr. Cooke has dealt with them, they take them home and boil them. Most of Mr. Cooke's eels come from Holland and Norway.

There is a magazine library rather like the one in Choumert Road, only they do not go in for penny dreadfuls in Shepherd's Bush. They have back numbers of *Vogue* and *The Tatler*, though there are often a few magazines with titles like *Thrilling Love*.

90

You will find a certain amount of second-hand furniture in this market, and an endless array of fenders and fire-guards, besides everything you could want for washing-day. A gipsy-like woman in fancy dress sits on a stool, waiting to tell fortunes. There are two or three cut-price cigarette and tobacco stalls.

I approached a large crowd that was standing round a sweet-maker. He was selling butter-drops, peppermints, and bright yellow and brown bull's-eyes. At the time he was brewing aniseed balls, and the smell of the aniseed stretched far across the market.

While he was shouting out a long rigmarole about his sweets, two small boys were going round with scoops, inviting the crowd to sample an aniseed ball.

Gradually I edged nearer, till I wriggled my way to the front of the crowd. It was then I made the gross error of speaking to him. My voice betrayed me, and he recognised somebody who did not really belong to that crowd. In a moment he had turned my visit to account and started a brawl round me. After all, a brawl is one of the best ways of advertising the stall. It draws a crowd quicker than anything.

"Listen, you chaps," he said. "I'm a tough guy. I talk out of the side of my mouth like this" (and he twisted his face to impress the many small boys in his audience). "Every time I'm locked up I say it's the bloody 'igh 'ats that ought to be locked up, not me. Look at 'er coming 'ere—look at 'er—I ask yer."

But I did not hear any more, for I had melted silently from their midst, and he was left still talking about me, imagining I was there, while the crowd swelled with all the "toughs" of Shepherd's Bush.

Well, I was afraid that might happen some time or other, and fortunately it only happened once. I should have really summed him up better than I did.

"I might say the Carlton Club in Pall Mall—there's a

letter from them—use this for all their carpets. Use it for everything, hats made like new—doesn't deteriorate—in a tin for sixpence."

A sandy-haired man selling a carpet-cleaning solution was demonstrating on one of the filthiest strips of carpet imaginable. As he worked on it the pattern came to light again, and he left a filth-covered strip to show it up. Sometimes he would pull an unpleasantly greasy trilby hat from his box of tricks and proceed to refurbish it with the carpet-cleaner, shaping it deftly on a block before he finished it off. The crowd bore this in silence, although many of them had hats like the one he was exhibiting as being well overdue for the carpet-cleaner.

"Whether or not you'll buy these I don't know," cried a toy-seller in rather laboured grammar. "Fivepence a box of crayons for a child—dolls three for twopence," he called, holding up another little box with dolls inside. "Tea-service for a child," he suggested, " and now I'm going to sell you something for nothing." And with great acclaim he held up an enormous dressed baby-doll (it really was a beauty). "I'm asking you where you can buy one like that for sixpence."

If it was as well-made at close quarters as it looked at a distance, somebody was going to be extremely lucky.

One stall is devoted entirely to selling workmen's overalls very cheaply. There is a sweet-seller called Papworth, who is generally to be found either eating his own sweets or chewing-gum. Anyway, his mouth works constantly, and he seems to enjoy it. At Morris's stall, stockings are 9d. a pair.

There is one very curious stall in Shepherd's Bush. It is called The Health Crusade, and the medically inclined gentleman who runs it is Mr. Geoffrey Carlisle. The stall is decorated with a few surgical instruments, some dressing receptacles, and a few pieces of laboratory apparatus. Two elegant-looking nurses in uniform dispense "The Cure," while Mr. Carlisle calls out all its merits. He also gives a demonstration with the laboratory apparatus on how acid

92

enters the body and forms rheumatism. Among other things, he claims to sell phosphorine for 6d. instead of the 15s. you pay in the chemist.

"There are twenty of us on the road altogether," he told me; "my brother went to Devizes yesterday."

Actually this dapper little man, who brings his bedside manner to the street market, does a great deal of good. He persuades hypochondriacal old ladies that a dose of his potion will restore them, and of course it has the desired effect.

Good-sized door-mats are 1s. 6d. or less in this street market, while baby-clothes are both attractive and cheap. Well-made little kid shoes for the baby are as cheap as 6d. a pair. You can get a solid leather music-case for 1s. A cot, complete with mattress and pillow, costs only 2s. 6d., and there are huge plain cupboards going for a few shillings.

"Look at that for a perfect figure," called a man, holding up a white china statue of a naked dancing-girl. He then began to auction it amid bawdy jokes from the crowd, until there was a bid of 9d.

At Betts's counter people go and order fritters and potato chips. Then they watch them cooked and carry them home hot in greaseproof paper.

David Leon is the most lively auctioneer in Shepherd's Bush. He sells a wonderful variety of cut-price goods, and he holds an auction that is worth hearing. While he is talking he flashes a rather Spanish smile on all his customers, and he certainly does an excellent trade.

"My goodness, Mrs. Maclean, you *are* clearing me out," he said to a woman who was carrying away a big collection of parcels when I arrived.

He held up a tin of liver salt. "Use a teaspoonful of this when you want, and it'll make your eyeballs stand out till you look so young you won't know yourselves. Bandages?" he proffered. "We sell a lot at Christmas-time with everybody knocking each other about. Come on now, if you haven't any money we'll take bus tickets. We don't take

93

pawn tickets: we've got too many of those ourselves. Hair-net? Want one, guv'nor? Oh, you're a bit bald 'eaded, I'm sorry."

Then he took up some loose tablets of soap. "Want a couple?" he called out to a woman at the back. "What? Don't you wash yerself? If you don't wash yerself it's no good selling you soap. Now, threepence for twenty envelopes, two pads of writing-paper, and a bottle of ink. Guaranteed to write fourteen thousand words out of one bottle."

As a writer I might have suggested that he was not being very wise in the matter, since I have yet to find a bottle of ink that would only provide for so few words. The one he held up was many times larger than that.

"Beads," he continued; "we sold fourteen thousand of these to that nudist colony at Hanworth the other day. Of course, the weather's been so bad they'll be buying a lot more soon. It's not yer money we want—it's yer custom. Ha'penny change? There ye are, me dear—yes, dear. Threepennorth and a bag. My goodness, you are doing yourself well. And now, Mrs. Leather-Bottom, what do you want?"

And so he babbles on, never at a loss for something to say, until his stall is empty and the crowd dispersed.

The outstanding feature of Shepherd's Bush Street Market is its pet store. The man who runs it is extraordinarily retiring, and usually leaves his assistants to look after the customers. But you can wander round at will and look at all the birds and fish for as long as you feel inclined.

Dozens of love-birds twitter prettily together in the cages. Canaries mingle their songs with the chirping of bullfinches. Parrots screech and talk. There are little fluffy chickens and grown-up hens, kittens, and several kinds of dogs, not to mention pigeons and cooing-doves. Good breeds of hens that normally cost 7s. 6d. a hen are 4s. 6d. there.

There is a fascinating collection of tropical fish, swimming in all shapes and sizes of aquariums. I stood for a long time by a glass tank of some fish called Chinese Moors that were being sold for 6s. each. They were black all over, and had

94

four tails, two sets of fins (like trailing black chiffon), and were hammer-headed, with bulging eyes. There were some tiny fish only about a quarter of an inch round, with transparent champagne-coloured skin and vivid blue stripes all round them. And there were many other lovely kinds of fish as well.

Apart from the actual birds, fish, and animals themselves, you can get every sort of food for them there as well, besides more ordinary things like bird-cages and dog-collars. If you are thinking of starting an aquarium, remember to go to the pet store—only give yourself plenty of time to enjoy looking round.

Dress materials are sold at Shepherd's Bush as well as in Berwick Market. One man has a notice on his stall that he buys old gold and silver. Presumably he sells it too. You can get four large-sized oranges for 1d. Assorted toffees are eight ounces for 5½d., and there are all sorts of cordials for 8d. a bottle.

Doris Baby Hut is a stall that has a tempting array of really good confectionery. Iced cakes, freshly made, that are normally 1s. 6d. to 2s. 6d., cost 5d. and 6d. Crumpets are two a penny. An enormous fruit-cake stuffed with plums is 1s. 6d., and large jam rolls are 4½d. instead of about 1s.

"My daddy's just gone out," said a very pretty little Jewish girl who was minding the stall. She told me her name was Lina Mussararno, and that she was thirteen and had no mother. Apparently all the cakes were made at their own bakery and brought out to the stall the same morning.

The Pen-Nib Man, as he wishes to be called, was busy writing four pages to advertise his pen, and he gave a flowery oration while he was doing it.

"No, I only come to this market," he told me in answer to my queries (I saw him at the Caledonian a few days later). "I'm not really a street-trader, I'm an actor—straight acting. I used to be on at Shepherd's Bush Empire. Give me three more weeks and I'll be top of your bill again."

He had a Scotch employer who stood by, watching to see how the pen-nibs were selling.

Husbands who accompany their wives to this street market while the time away at the pin tables, until the shopping is finished. One enterprising stall-holder sells his goods on a gaming-table.

Then I came across the Shepherd's Bush Lady Godiva, with long brown tresses reaching, literally, almost to her feet. It is quite the thing to stare in a street market, and I felt she was probably accustomed to it, for I went up and stared at her ruthlessly to see if I could find any joins half-way down her tresses. But there was no join, and it was certainly not a wig, so after that I felt inclined to stay and listen. On the stall in front of her were a number of little bottles of liquid and a bundle of pamphlets.

"I'll tell you for why," she was saying. "This is what happens—you get dandruff. I won't keep you long. But tell me, how do you wash and dry your hair? You wash it in soap and water, then dry it before the fire, and that takes out all the natural grease. You can say what you like, I don't mind. Mine's not been washed for five weeks and look at it."

She ran a comb through it and held a bunch of her hair towards the customers. "See, it's quite clean, but it's still got the natural grease, and it's not lost its colour. I'm very particular what I buy. Ninety-nine per cent. of the shampoo powders you buy contain carbohydrate of soda."

"Spell it," interrupted a male cynic in the crowd who had just finished an inquisitive stare at her hair.

She gave him a withering look and went on.

"If you have dandruff, get rid of it. Only don't wash your hair in soap and water or use shampoos. I'll tell you for why . . ."

What does Lady Godiva do with her hair when she is not at the market? Can she put it up, or does she wear it in plaits? And if she puts it up, can she wear a hat?

I longed to ask her those questions, but I did not get a chance. No one does.

96

Club Row

ARE you fond of animals? Then come to Club Row on a Sunday morning. But you must be really fond of them—fond enough to forget such things as pedigrees and pure breeding, and love them just for themselves.

Club Row is a turning off the Bethnal Green Road, not far from Liverpool Street Station, and it only becomes a street market on Sunday mornings, when the stalls have to pack up by one o'clock. You can hear it long before you get there. Dogs bark, while puppies whine and yelp. There are parrots screeching, and hundreds of birds twittering, besides the men selling "bird warblers," who each go about with one of these little whistles in their mouth to advertise what it can do.

Hens squawk with indignation at being pulled out of their pens and handled. Ridiculously, a cock crows now and then, piercing the rest of the uproar and making the whole place sound more like a farmyard than ever. There are ducks quacking plaintively, geese, turkeys, pigeons, and plenty of kittens. Beside them all, the humans seem strangely silent.

The first view of the market is a dense crowd of men, most of them wearing mufflers and caps. They are typical of the crowd that moves round all the East End street markets, and they are called "the boys." All the time they lurk silently and slowly round the stalls, watching, brooding. Sometimes one of them will suddenly quicken his footsteps and move away. Here and there they gather into groups and speak to each other in low voices.

Nobody knows who they are or what they do. And nobody dare ask them. Many of them are probably street-bookies, or touts from some of the stalls. You may sometimes see them making signs to each other as you go by, or they might follow you a little way, but not beyond their own purlieus.

In Club Row they are interspersed with men holding dogs on leads and chains. These men move in and out of the crowd, each trying to draw attention to their charge and making people stop and discuss its merits.

It is a sad thing to watch. I saw several of these dogs looking with scared, puzzled eyes at the people round them. Some of them strained at the leash till their throats gurgled from the stain—as though they would flee in terror from the men who held them. The little dogs shivered miserably, more from fear than cold. Some of them stood with sagging legs and downcast heads, as if they had lost all faith in life. Once I saw a brave Alsatian fight its captor until it had torn its head from a tight collar, and it vanished through the crowd like a hunted fox. They were too amazed to follow in pursuit, for it was strong and hurled them aside as though nothing would stop its flight.

" 'Ullo, 'ee's slipped 'is collar!" somebody commented, with a whoop of excitement. The lad who had been holding it tried to follow, but the Alsatian was out of sight. He was left still holding the chain and blinking stupidly, while he wondered what to do about it all. Probably by that time it had been caught and was being sold by some one else. I almost prayed that it had got away.

A man walked past with two very young puppies in his coat. Wisely he left their soft little crumpled faces to plead for a new home. He did not try and press people into buying them.

I spoke to a man who had a large collection of puppies in clean sawdust-filled pens. He said he sold about twenty of them every Sunday. Most of them were difficult to name as belonging to any particular breed, but they were well-kept and very lovable. Children clustered round the pens, stroking the puppies and talking to them. And when they ran away there were always fresh children to take their place.

"Genuine Aberdeen terrier," called a man, picking up a

98

little brown-and-black puppy of extremely questionable parentage. "Collies," called another man, selling a litter that made one think also of spaniels.

There is a rumour that people have been known to buy a dog in Club Row, and then in all innocence they have taken the precaution of giving it a bath. After that their little "black Scottie" came out a mottled tawny colour, looking every bit the mongrel he was before he was so discreetly dyed.

An unfortunate Pekingese was being used as a model for a stall of dogs' toilet requisites. For the entire morning it had to stay on the stall and be submitted to a succession of dry shampoos, while the stall-holder bellowed out the merits of his powder. "That's the way to move all vermin; cleans the skin—keeps away mange and scotches fleas." He also sold dogs' brushes and an assortment of combs.

Mr. J. Lewis sells bird-sand for 1d. a pint, and all kinds of canary food and bird seed. There are also bottles of bird tonic, costing 3d. each, and he has pieces of cuttlefish "to help a bird to keep its upper bill short." His canary food is 4d. a pint, and linnet food and finch food is the same price. He says he can speak half a dozen languages. An extraordinary number of stall-holders are anxious to claim that achievement, but, excluding Mr. Lewis himself, I should not like to put any of them to the test.

"The best yer money can buy," he calls. "Everything fer yer canary. Now, buyers, come along. Now, gentlemen, come along. I've twenty years' experience in veterinary surgery. Ask anything you like and I'll answer it. Tell you anything you like to ask. Canary food, linnet food, goldfish food."

Dart-stalls are plentiful in Club Row. One had a large notice on it:

"THE ORIGINAL CLUB ROW DART-STALL

We're not champion dart-players,
But we've champion darts."

The dart-stalls seem to do very good trade.

One man had some little black puppies in a box, and they all had pale-blue bows round their necks. The bows made them an extra attraction, and a mob of children were fighting to get near enough to stroke them. An old man nearby was rather surly about letting people look at his canaries, and he was asking a very high price for them compared with the other stall-holders.

Not only are there stalls with canaries and love-birds for sale, but there are several big bird-stores down the street, which join in and become part of the street market. Cages hang right up the walls outside, while they are piled high inside the stores.

In spite of the dingy street and the rough crowd surging round, the birds still twitter prettily the whole morning. Here and there a moulting parrot sits gloomily on its perch, looking as though it was just waiting to die. But on the whole the birds look extraordinarily well kept and well cared for. Most of them are in beautiful condition.

Apart from a superfluity of canaries and budgerigars there are linnets, bullfinches, and I saw a lovely Virginia nightingale being sold for 8s. Canaries are marked 8s. a pair, but everybody in Club Row is open to a bargain—at any rate later in the morning if not at the beginning.

Bird-cages as well as their tenants are very cheap down there. You can get a big breeding-cage, well fitted out for a canary's family life, for the modest sum of 3s. 6d. or less.

There was a monkey chained to the roof of a cage full of budgerigars in one bird-store. I think he was there more to attract attention than to be bought by a customer, though the bird-man did try and sell him to me.

"All complaints fer yer sick animals," called a man with his stall decked out as a complete animal dispensary. "I've got everything you want. Any questions you want to ask about yer sick animals, don't mind asking me. I'll answer 'em all. Condition powders—worm powders!" he added

100

menacingly to a lad who had been standing round for some time without buying anything. The lad took the hint and moved away into safety. Most of the usual dog powders were only 2d. at that stall. There was a complete, if slightly embarrassing, list of all the ailments he cured for a shilling a treatment.

"Henry the Plater," as he is called, is a man who sells a mysterious preparation for making brass fenders look like chromium. Most of the street-traders sell their wares by gradually knocking the price down. But Henry is different.

"Now, I've bin down here fer years," he'll say. "The price is going up, not going down. I told you last week this would be the last time that I was asking only a shilling a bottle. Well, now, this is the last time. A half-crown bottle for one shilling only. Never no more."

"The bitches don't get enough grass, that's the trouble," one man said to another. Conversations generally run on dogs or birds in Club Row.

A man with several crates of hens was holding a large white fowl by its legs, while a woman customer felt it and pinched it shamelessly in front of the crowd. The white fowl squawked in protest, till eventually she nodded her head, and, taking hold of it, she crammed it into a fish-bag and carried it home.

Spotted scarves, really quite good ones, are 6d. each, and a man sells "music strings" for several instruments at cut prices. All kinds of sweet-sales take place from the big stalls, clearing off quantities of toffee and chocolates, down to the pathetic old men who are selling a few twopenny-size bars of milk chocolate for 1d. each. They have the bars laid out on the dusty boards, and keep fingering them all the time they are calling out.

I saw two stalls selling a variety of new caps for 1s. 6d. each. Probably "the boys" manage to get them for less. They were just the kind they wear.

Mrs. Miller has the quaintest stall of anybody. She sells

plain wooden chair-legs, "three shillings for four, dearie," and little bits of carving for 1d., 2d., and 4½d. So, when their chairs give way, or they decide to make the banisters look more ornate, the people of Club Row go to Mrs. Millar. Very likely she has a husband in the background who makes the spare chair-legs and does the carving.

There were plenty of pigeons for sale. "Ask Pa," said a small boy who was minding some, when I asked him the price. But "Pa" looked so forbidding I decided to let it rest.

The "bird-warbler" men are everywhere. Threepence was the price of the bird-warblers, and the men themselves certainly excelled in playing them. They would imitate nearly a dozen different bird-calls in succession, and they always kept their lips parted to show how the "warbler" should be held.

The man who had a large crate of grey geese, which he was selling at 4s. 6d. each, told me he sold live turkeys for 6s. each, and ducks for 2s. 6d.

Then I found old Emerick with his tame rabbits. He has them running about loose on his stall, and they are so tame that they do not try to run away. He is very gentle and kind with them, and obviously tames them himself. You can buy them for 2s. to 2s. 6d. each. I believe he hates parting with them, and every time a rabbit is sold it wrings his heart. At the end of the morning, if there are any left he pushes them into old suit-cases and carries them back home.

I saw a stall piled high with new motor-tyres and hot-water bottles. It would have been interesting to know the reduction on them, but a peep at the stall-holder terrified me so much that I did not inquire.

Quite a thick crowd had gathered round one man on the pavement, and I pushed my way through it to see what he was doing. He had little cages of tame mice, fitted with all kinds of playthings for them—just two cages and two pairs of mice. He was selling them for 1s. 6d. a pair with the cage.

102

Club Row

"How much did you pay for those?" I asked a small girl in the crowd. She was carrying a cake-box full of little yellow chickens. I could see them through the cellulose top. But she only stared at me with a brooding suspicion and said nothing. Even the smallest children in Club Row have learned to trust nobody.

"Two-and-six a dozen," said a man standing near her. He was probably a tout for the chicken-seller, so I imagine they cost less than that.

Henry Bradley is one of the nicest things in Club Row. He is a dear old pensioner who stands on the pavement selling chickweed for canaries. "Penny a bunch," he says quietly to the people who pass by. "See, you can hang it up in the cage," he says, holding up a succulent piece.

It probably sounds ridiculous to country-folk that anybody should be foolish enough to pay for chickweed. But Club Row is very far from green fields—to those who cannot afford the journey.

Henry is a very happy person, for he spends the week roaming in the fields, picking chickweed. And then on Sundays he goes to Club Row. It gives him a lot of pleasure, and some country air—and it makes that old-age pension go just a little farther.

Although the market virtually shuts at one o'clock, the police are still busy at one-thirty, urging the stall-holders to pack up and leave. And the crowd stays on. There are still birds to be sold, so the bird-men have touts who go round trying to sell them off long after the stalls are cleared away.

Each man will carry what appears to be an innocent parcel in a brown paper carrier. Then, when he has a crowd round him, thick enough to hide him from the police, he will pull down the brown paper carrier and reveal the cage with its little feathered tenants.

Puppies are taken round underneath their overcoats. Dogs are still led about on chains mended with bits of string. They

103

are only taking them home, they would say if they were questioned. But they change hands all the same, and that is probably when there are some ready bargains.

You, too, will be there long after one o'clock—lingering to the last.

Hildreth Street

IN a turning off the Balham High Street there is a homely little street market, which the Balham housewives can visit every day of the week. This is Hildreth Street.

The first corner stall is a lavish flower-stall, presided over by tall Mrs. Pearson, who dominates and mothers the rest of the stall-holders all down the street. It is she who first welcomes you, and she will introduce you to the others and tell you who is who in Hildreth Street.

Her tulips are 1s. 6d. a dozen at times when the shops are charging 2s. 6d., narcissus 2d. a bunch, and daffodils 8d. a dozen. "Fresh flowers," she calls, but not very loudly, for nobody shouts in this street market.

Mrs. Cummings sells heads of celery three for 2d., bananas two a penny, pears 4d. a pound, and grapes 4d. a pound, and she has 1½d. baskets of mustard and cress. I thought she had the best display of fruit in the market, and she runs the stall with the help of her curly-headed sixteen-year-old son, Bill Cummings.

In this market you can buy pineapple by the slice, instead of having to spend a small fortune buying a whole one.

Next door to the Cummings's stall there is Mr. Orrey's vegetable-stall. He has been at this stall in Hildreth Street for thirty years, and he says the market only came into existence forty years ago. To begin with, his prices are not as a whole lower than the shops, but he does have a clear-out every Saturday night, when he lets things go for less. "I like having a clear-out even if they do go for less than they cost," he said, "because then I can be sure of having everything fresh."

One stall makes a speciality of clothes-pegs—two dozen for 2½d.

If ever there was a "guide, philosopher, and friend" in any street market it is golden-hearted Mrs. Perry. I should like to be able to send for her whenever I had a fit of depression. She looks a little like Marion Lorne, has ebullient spirits, a joke for every one, and a wonderful philosophy that goes with a remarkably intelligent outlook. In fact, she does one good.

Evidently I am not alone. Mrs. Perry has more friends than it would be possible to count, and customers go to see her just as much as to buy her salads. Many of them send her presents and write her letters when they go abroad.

In winter she sits beside an oil-stove, with an east wind blowing up Hildreth Street and her salads sometimes frozen to the stall. But she is laughing and joking with every one, and people who are not buying salads stop to tell her their news. She stays by the stall all day, and before that she has been to market and done all the buying. Salads mean there is quite a heavy task to be done "cleaning the stuff," and that takes her husband a full day to do.

Not long ago Mrs. Perry used to drive her own horse and cart to market every morning. But the pony has grown too old for work. She was in the market before the licensing days, and ran with the best of them to secure her pitch when the policeman blew his whistle.

"I was younger in those days," she chuckled, "but if it came to pushing a barrow and running fast now, I think I should be one of the losers. There was often a free fight over a pitch. The policeman had his hands full, I can tell you, until we got settled down! Fortunately there weren't many customers about so early. The few there were found it great fun watching. But we didn't care a tinker's continental for anybody until we got our pitches safely."

"You know, I've got a lot of customers who often go abroad," she continued, "and whenever they go they write to me. One lady sent me a postcard from the Brussels Exhibition. But she wrote it in French, so all I could read was the

106

address. Another lady travelled to China and she brought my little girl a Chinese doll in native wedding-dress. The same lady brought me a work-box from Burma, made by the Mongolians.''

I suggested she might like to go abroad herself.

"Yes, but I'd always want to come back again," she said. "I've been to France for a week-end, but I wasn't struck on it. It was funny what happened there. I was standing looking up at the Casino, when suddenly some one crept up behind me and whispered, 'You're a long way from Balham, Ma!' And there was one of my customers. Wouldn't you think I could hide in France? But I love being in the market. People are all so dandy and they're just fine, though it's a hard life in winter. I used to have to wash three kids and take them to the nursery before I started at the stall in the morning. And then people talk to *me* about getting through their housework. Why, I was scrubbing the kitchen floor at half-past eleven last night!"

In spite of all her hard work Mrs. Perry looks twenty years younger than she really is, and so obviously enjoys her life. She belongs to the local Conservative Association, and sometimes speaks at their meetings. She stood up and pleaded with the crowd outside the hall just before the election, and before that she had worked hard, canvassing.

"But I'm afraid I shall never make a good speaker; I haven't got the education," she said modestly. "I've never been to school in me life. Though it's meeting other folks that teaches you most, I think."

And to support this she told me a story. "There was a lad who tried for a job cleaning a shed. But they wouldn't have him because he couldn't read or write. So he got a few shillings together and started street-trading. Then he did so well that he opened a shop, and then another shop. And he'd got quite a bit of money by then, so he took it to the bank and opened a bank account. And the bank manager said, 'It's a pity, you know. If only you'd had some education you

107

would have gone far.' And that lad pointed across the road to the shed and said, 'If I'd 'a been educated I should still be cleaning that shed.' Wasn't that dandy?"

Yes, and wasn't Mrs. Perry dandy? You must go and see her.

Before we leave our flying visit to Hildreth Street you must meet "Tommy" Sanders. He has two stalls, with over a hundred oddments on them—all things that are dear to housewives—beads, buttons, shoe-laces, teaspoons, floor-cloths, dusters, pins, and just everything you can imagine you might want for running the house. He compares with the haberdashery department in a big store, but he is more than that, for he sells many more things than a haberdasher, and they are a good deal cheaper.

East Street, Walworth Road

It was Friday night in East Street, and women poured into the street market to do their shopping. They had just collected their husbands' wages, for last week's money had not lasted long enough to buy to-night's dinner. Gusts of wind frolicked with the stalls, billowing their canvas roofs and snatching stray pieces of paper. There had been showers all day, and the rain still gleamed in the cracks between the cobbles. In the daytime rain-water looks dreary and cold, but the street-lamps picked it out and made it sparkle and reflect them till the street seemed full of myriads of shining lights.

Here and there a stall-holder cried out his wares. Children played up and down the street, pushing packing-cases over the cobbles and screaming shrilly to each other to get out of the way. Their faces were drawn and tired, yet their eyes still glittered with mischief and excitement. They ran wild all the evening, for their mothers were far too busy to put them to bed. Sometimes they would get sworn at by a stall-holder for knocking things off a stall. And they would run away, only to steal back and pick up a fallen apple. There was gossip occasionally, and here and there an empty stall. Prosperity is a stranger in the Walworth Road district, and some of the stall-holders cannot make ends meet. Sometimes the winter grips an old chest, and then there is another empty stall while the owner is away ill.

Silk stockings were 9d. and 1s. a pair that night. Ones with a notice, "slightly imperfect," were 6d. a pair. I passed a butcher who sang songs to bring customers to his stall. People need cheering up in East Street, and it is the cheerful stall-holders who draw all the trade.

Old Mrs. McGuinness sells "taters" for a top price of 1d. a pound, and you can bargain with her for greens towards

109

the end of the evening. The potatoes will keep, so you have less hope of bargaining over them.

House shoes are 2s. 11d. a pair. You can get a half-pound of sweets for 1d. "Chocolate throw-outs" are the same price. In most of the other street markets they would disguise them in festive-looking boxes and sell them for 2s. But they are far less ruthless in East Street.

There was a pathetic little stall with just a few carrots on it, and a very ragged old woman trying to sell them. She had not priced them. She was going to fight and pray for all she could get. Many of the stall-holders wash and scrub their carrots till they look a spotless bright pink. But she had not even troubled to rub the earth from them, and soap and water was a luxury she could not afford.

The most popular person in East Street is Mrs. Rumble. It was a long time before I could tear myself from her stall. She simply radiates fun and good humour, is ready to joke with all her customers, and, besides being an excellent sales-woman, she does a brisk trade the whole time.

"What do yer want to-day, old dear?" she said, turning to a very footsore old woman. "Give us yer list and we'll see fer a start." And the old woman let her take her shopping-list from her trembling old fingers. While Mrs. Rumble read it out, "Bill," her young assistant, fetched the goods and popped them in the old woman's shopping-bag. Then there was the checking up to be done. Again the old woman left it to Mrs. Rumble, whose quick brain did the sum for her, and then she went away. She was so old and hazy that anybody could have swindled her only too easily. But Mrs. Rumble is trusted as well as liked by all her customers, and the old lady knew she was perfectly safe with her.

Then came another customer who could not read her shopping-list, but this time it was a little girl-toddler with a basket almost the same size as herself.

"Four of sugar," Mrs. Rumble called out briskly, while Bill bustled round for her. "Three of starch. A large Mili-

110

tary pickle, Bill. Tin of salt, duck. That's right. That's all now. Good-night, my darling." And the child went away, looking rather like an ant carrying an egg, because the basket was so large and heavy for her.

Next moment Mrs. Rumble was trying to put a woman's accounts in order. "One-and-eleven and two-three—now two-and-threepence—I make it twopence less than what you do." And she endeavoured to prove her arithmetic, while the woman stared in helpless admiration, not really taking anything in at all.

"What was that other one?" asked Bill suddenly, who for the moment had got behind with an order.

"I told you, dearie," called Mrs. Rumble—"sixpennorth of salt and a sixpenny chunk of pineapple, duck.

"Now what d'you want?" she asked, turning to a small boy who was tugging at her skirt. But he had forgotten what his mother had told him to buy.

"What yer sucking then?" asked Mrs. Rumble, to fill in time.

He opened his mouth to exhibit its contents.

"My 'at, look at yer mouth! and just look at yer tongue, dear!" she exclaimed, when she saw the brilliant scarlet effect of a rather vivid-coloured jube-jube.

Then he suddenly remembered; yes, he had got a shopping-list, and he held it out on the end of one finger which was so sticky that the paper adhered to it of its own accord.

"There you are, dear," she said, whisking up the shopping-list. "One of lifebuoy—bar of sunlight soap. Oh, bend down and get me some more sunlight soap from that box underneath," she pleaded to Bill. "Excuse me," he teased, "but it'd do you good to bend down. Do yer figure good."

Mrs. Rumble bridled. "My figure's good enough without bending down." And Bill dived underneath the stall and came up again with the lifebuoy soap.

"Bill, give me four and a half unsweetened milk, please. You'll find some in the warehouse on top there, duck. There's a lot in there," she added.

Mrs. Rumble has groceries for 4d. an item when they are 6d. in the shops. Jams are 1d. and 2d. cheaper, and she has 1d. toilet soaps and almost every line that any big grocer keeps can be got at her stall. She is a strong, healthy young woman with a delightful smile, and she is the most brisk and competent person I have ever come across.

"Come along, ladies," she calls, "give us yer purses. 'Ere ye are, girls. Pick up what you like, I'll soon tell you the price." And when she is short of things to cry out, she engages in a little playful banter with Bill, who is nearly as lively as she is herself.

She is known affectionately among her customers as "Ada," and she has been in the market eighteen years. When she was nineteen she used to stand up on a soap-box and call out cheery street-cries with the best of them. Her husband does all the buying, so he leaves the stall to the care of Ada and Bill.

"Customers come up and ask me 'Is this good?' " she told me. "An' I say, 'If it wasn't good I shouldn't sell it.' Then they pick up a tin of peas an' say 'What is it?' An' I say, 'Peas,' as though they couldn't see fer themselves! They even come up and ask me the time, but that isn't much good, because I never know it meself. You see that dear old lady there? She came and bought two tins of soup. Then she came along next day and said, ''Ow do yer use that soup?' So I tells her. An' then she 'as to come to me after 'er dinner and tell me what a good stew she made out of it!"

Gibbs's stall has big strips of coco-nut matting for 2s. 6d. You can get a whole floor-covering for 9d., not linoleum but a composition that looks very like it. In East Street people take their floor carpet away and lay it themselves, but if you are not as handy as they are, Mr. Gibbs will come and lay it for you at a charge of 2d. a yard. Door-mats run from 3d. to 2s. 6d. each, and a large strip of Chinese matting is only 8d.

People who do not like paying 7s. 6d. to 12s. 6d. a dozen

112

for their oysters at fashionable oyster-bars in the West End should go to Mrs. Clayton in East Street and get them for 1s. 6d. a dozen. Hers are not Whitstable oysters, they are Portuguese, but they are very good all the same. She also sells cockles, whelks, and mussels, and customers can demolish them on the spot, complete with the necessary condiments to go with them.

We asked her if she'd ever found a pearl inside any of her oysters.

"No, duck, I wish I could!" she said. "I'd retire and go away and lead a gay life."

While she spoke she was busy shelling mussels and popping them into jars of pickle, ready to be sold at 6d. a jar. By the evening she had a pile of mussel-shells beside her that almost reached up to her waist.

If you see a broad figure, a pair of high black boots, and a smiling face underneath a man's soft cap—that is Mrs. Dress. She has a supply of very good vegetables at really low prices. Her cooked beets are "twopence a lot of four," and you get four beauties for your money. Leeks are two a penny. Her husband pickles onions for her in a shed close by, and she sells them on the stall.

Mr. Money, who also sells vegetables, claims to be the veteran of East Street Market. He is seventy-four, and has worked in the market ever since he could stand.

There is a china stall where you can buy odd cups. Like most of the street markets they do not keep many saucers, because hardly anybody uses them.

"Twopence a pound, best apples. 'Ere ye are, twopence a pound, best eaters," called a woman stall-holder in a high cracked voice, as she held them out in a scale-pan to the passing crowd. The ones in the scale-pan looked very good.

Mrs. Priddy was sitting at her salad-stall nibbling celery. She looked so cheerful I stayed to talk to her.

"Lettuces, twopence each," she called out, in between mouthfuls of celery; "fresh and nice. Nice lettuce, dear?"

113

I remarked on her liking for celery. "Oh yes, duck, I only eat the top," she said, rather guiltily. "I shall eat a bit of the middle later on," she added, with a mischievous twinkle. "Penny each, celery," she called, while the pile of celery was rapidly dwindling, more from her doing than her customer's. "Rhubarb! good for the blood."

There were pickled onions for sale too, and I asked her if she prepared them.

"No, duck, the guv'nor does it. 'E don't like the stall work, so 'e amuses 'imself picklin'."

Then I caught sight of a glass of whisky sitting behind a large horseradish, and I pointed at it to tease her.

"Yes, duck, I've just 'ad it fetched me." And her eyes twinkled at the thought of it.

East Street does not stay awake much after nine on Friday night. There is still Saturday night to come, when every one goes crazy and nobody goes to bed before eleven. I left while the street market was still vividly awake. It would have been a sad sight to see it packing up. Instead, I went away with the cries ringing in my ears, the children screaming and playing, and the rain still sparkling under the lamplight, in the cracks between the cobbles.

Portobello Road

IN the remotest end of Portobello Road, Notting Hill Gate, there is quite a long, housewifely street market. This is one of the poorest districts in West London, and not every stall is to be chosen for shopping, but there are a few with really good, clean bargain food. In any case, the characters are rather amusing.

"Oh, shut up, duck; come along and have a drink and forget it," said one old woman, trying to console another whose "old man" had apparently left her high and dry.

Gough's butcher's stall has meat 6½d. a pound less than the shops, and it is cheaper still after five o'clock in the evening, when he holds an auction. You can get a very good large leg of lamb there for 2s. 9d. down to 2s. 4d.

I stopped to talk to round, chuckling Mrs. Brooks, who has been there thirty years, and looks wonderfully young for her age.

"I'm sixty, dear," she told me, "and I've got four children and ten grandchildren. My son 'ee's the gov'nor at this stall."

Her fruit is excellent and very cheap. Greens, three pounds for 2d.; grape-fruit, 1½d. each, are only two of the many bargains she has to offer.

"I generally 'ave me scales so bright yer can see yer face in 'em," she apologised, "but to-day the rain's gorn and spoilt 'em horrible. Trade's pretty fair," she told me, "but it's best on Friday afternoon. We stay open till nine in summer and nine-thirty in winter."

Then I came across a strange figure, dressed in a torn fur coat held together with safety-pins, a man's cap, and high, seaworthy-looking black boots. She was sitting on a sugar-box with her back to her vegetable-stall, busily sucking her

115

teeth and picking them with her finger-nails. I told her I wanted to put her in a book.

"I can't read, dear," she said, with an abandoned giggle. "Taters a penny a pound," she called out.

Then she rescued something she had been trying to suck from her teeth, and took it out to inspect it. This rather handicapped our conversation, and I went on to see Mrs. Poulsen, who has a fruit-stall.

"Everythin' good and ripe," called Mrs. Poulsen, standing before her array of fruit. "I've bin here since I was about seven year old, and I've got a salad-stall as well," she told me proudly.

"Nice lettuce, all 'earts," she called, to give the salad-stall a boost.

"I say, I must take me blackboard down, mustn't I?" She threw a guilty glance at her mourning-board which was still there some days after the King's funeral. Probably it is still there now, because I think she was just a little proud of it.

Mrs. Pike is the gayest stall-holder in Portobello Road, and she just loves a joke with a customer. She is a short, round little figure, with a face wreathed in smiles, and she has all the latest gossip at her finger-tips.

"All fresh and nice, guaranteed sound fruit," she calls out whenever she has time between a bit of gossip. As a matter of fact, it is good fruit, and she does not try to push the price up if you look like having a full purse.

"Some of the customers are so funny, they're that suspicious," she laughed. "They come an' say, 'You're *sure* there's no rotten ones, aren't you? *Sure* it's the right weight?' An' they ask, 'How much *are* yer apples?' when they've got a price ticket on 'em plain as me name's Pike. Children come an' ask me fer 'a ha'penny apple and can yer give us *two*?' 'Course one 'as to be kind to 'em. We've got children ourselves—one's seven and one's eight.

"Me husband does the buying," she told me later. "An' we have to look round to get the things just a bit cheaper than what we sell 'em for. That's our life, isn't it?

116

"I 'ave to call to all the men. Every one that comes by—we don't know 'em, but we call out," she giggled archly.

Then came a long story of how somebody had once taken her photograph at the stall.

"There was I, 'aving a bit of a joke with two of me lady friends, and we was all laughin' fit to split. An' he took us when we weren't looking, and next day he come and showed it to me. He'd caught me just as I was doubled up with laughing, and I'd pushed me 'at back over me 'ead like I do when I'm having a good laugh," and she pushed her hat back to show me. "I didn't half look a sketch, I can just tell you."

But after this description I had to leave her, because the customers were getting impatient to be served.

Mrs. Pike was a welcome ray of happiness in a market that was otherwise depressing, and just a little bit sordid compared with most of the others.

Hoxton Street

PAT is twelve years old, Irish, and has bright red hair, a freckled face, and a very disarming smile. He calls his young mother "Ann," and provides her with a gallant, though fitful protection, while his greatest craze is an alarming collection of guns. His armoury comprises about fifteen different weapons, ranging from field-guns to pistols, tanks, machine-guns, and air-guns. He seldom goes about unarmed, and he usually has at least two pistols hidden inside his belt, besides another one in his pocket.

It was with Pat that I went to Hoxton Street, and his mother came with us too.

On week-days this street market is mainly composed of a number of food-stalls, but on Saturday about a hundred extra stalls are fitted in between the others. During Christmas-time about fifty of these are toy-stalls, for some of those that sell other lines the rest of the year blossom into toy-stalls for December. But of the genuine toy-stalls there are generally about twenty that set up every Saturday all the year round.

Hoxton Street is only a short distance from Shoreditch Church, and the street market has been there for about a hundred years or more. There was an old charter for "Hoxton Market," and that market was originally in a tiny square called Hoxton Square, which is now used for parking cars. When the market tended to grow too big for the square, it was moved into Pitfield Street, and then it grew still larger and it had to be moved again to Hoxton Street. Most of the stalls that are there now have been handed down through the family for three generations or more.

Hoxton Street has a reputation for being wonderfully cheap, for it caters for very poor people. Shoppers come there from many of the surrounding districts. The market inspectors say that it is full of very kind-hearted folk, who are always ready to help each other even when they are so hard up themselves.

During the week all the business is done before midday, and most of the stalls close down after one o'clock. But on Saturdays, when all the toys are out, the street market is the brightest spot in Shoreditch, and its liveliest moment is Saturday afternoon when all the children are out of school. Another busy time is Sunday morning.

When Pat went street-marketing he had to have his pockets well fortified with sweets, and of course as usual he was armed to the teeth. In the train he regaled us with a lurid description of a cowboy serial he had seen on the films. There had been a good deal of shooting in it, and excitement danced in his eyes as he retold every detail that had happened. But when we got to Hoxton Street everything else faded before the feast of toys, and even cowboys were forgotten.

There was a strange little theatre on wheels that belonged to a roving stall-holder called Edward Whiterod. "Jack Payne and his Boys" was painted on the outside, and inside, on the little stage, was a complete model jazz band. He told us he made all the "boys" out of old Bournville cocoa-tins, and the whole thing only took him about six months to complete.

That part of the pavement was fairly quiet just then, so we put a penny in the slot to hear the "boys" play the band.

Mr. Whiterod pulled a gramophone needle out of his pocket, and collected a record from somewhere under his little theatre. Then he disappeared behind it, and put on "The Music goes Round and Round," which was then a brand-new dance tune. I thought that when he put it on the figures would remain rigid and we should only be hearing a pennyworth of gramophone record. But instead, directly the record began playing, all the "boys" came to life and played their instruments. The man with a double bass drew his

120

bow to and fro across the strings, the pianist thumped on the piano, and the conductor beat time with his baton, while all the others played their various instruments.

And they were once only a few old cocoa-tins.

"At night-time it all lights up," said Mr. Whiterod while the music was still playing.

Just then I looked round, and found we were completely surrounded by a big crowd of children and just as many grown-ups.

The news had spread like lightning. Somebody had put a penny in the money-box, and they had all gathered round to take advantage of it. One small girl had just got to the front by butting her way through with her head. She was resting her stick of liquorice against my skirt while she stared at the jerking tin figures. I spoke to her, but she did not hear. The "boys" were holding her spellbound.

Mr. Whiterod had a nice kind face, and I think he understood about pocket-money.

"I used to be a fitter—that was really my trade," he told me. "I've bin a boiler-fitter, a hydraulic fitter, and a carpenter's fitter—all kinds—and I've even made gramophone records. Stand back! Say, you'll pull it over," he called out anxiously to some small boys.

They had arrived rather late, and, failing to get a good place in the crowd, they were trying to jostle the stall along into a position of better advantage to themselves. It had to be done by falling against it so as to look like an accident, and when they grew bolder they began to move the stall several inches along the road. But Mr. Whiterod ran round and scared them away, for fear they should put one of the "boys" out of action or scratch the record by jogging it when it was playing.

"The worst of it is so many of them come, but they don't many of them pay a penny for it," he said. But I had seen that this was only too true.

I enjoyed that penny entertainment more than I can say.

121

Many of the stall-holders in Hoxton Street are only called by nicknames after their trade. One of the best known of them was an old man called "Old Irony," who had a stall loaded with old iron. But they say he died a few months ago, and so far there has been no second old-iron merchant to take his place.

"Look at that, if you don't mind!" said Pat, surveying the cat's-meat-stall with some distaste. "We had a cat's-meat man up our way in Alperton who used to carry round six-pennorth of cat's meat on little wooden sticks and sell 'em in the street. And when he walked along there used to be about fifty cats following him an' all."

The live-eel-stall did not appear to repel him in the same way. In fact, he stopped to peep into the bowls, and watched them wriggling with interest.

"I like twisting them in knots," he said revoltingly, and he went on to give a garnished description of how many eels his mother used to eat, while she protested hotly that it was untrue.

There was an old man who had his stall littered with second-hand teddy-bears and battered tin trumpets. But there were three recently emptied beer-glasses standing by the toys, so we did not encourage Pat to talk to him. The whole contents of the stall looked as though it was scarcely enough to buy three glasses of beer.

Even the grown-up china-stall was not entirely grown-up, for it sold very pretty little dolls' tea-sets for 2d. a set. It also had pencil-cases and scrubbing-brushes, and Pat's quick eyes picked out some toy saxophones that he was longing to test.

I just had time for a sneaking glance at some of the food bargains. Tomatoes were 2½d. a pound and bananas five for 2d. And then I saw a fish-stall which claimed to have red-spotted plaice (the spots denote better quality). But was it an illusion that one of the spots was beginning to run?

We listened to a little boy telling a stall-holder that he

122

was going to play football that afternoon. He was so small that he could have been no more than four or five years old.

"What are you going to play?" asked the stall-holder good-naturedly.

"Goalkeeper," said the little boy, throwing out his chest.

The stall-holders are all very kind to the children, and extremely patient with mischievous small boys.

They sell salt in Hoxton Street, and there are stalls presided over by old women with saws, who saw off a large hunk for a customer and only charge them 1d. or 2d.

"Hi, just look at the mouth of her! That little girl's lips are thick with red," said Pat, scandalised at a little girl who had borrowed her mother's lipstick and applied it inartistically to her small mouth.

"Four a penny, squeaking dolls," called Mr. Jones. But Pat looked at them scornfully. What is a mere squeak compared with the report of a gun!

Apparently this stall-holder sells a different line of things each day, but he keeps to the one line while the day lasts.

One old man, the other side, had such a crowd of children round his stall that we could not see many of his toys.

"Just look at all those children!" exclaimed Pat's mother. "Did you ever see the like of it! Isn't it marvellous where they all come from?"

"They might all be his, for all we know," said Pat innocently.

"Oh, Pat!" rebuked his mother, but her reproach collapsed into a giggle half-way through.

But Pat was staring at a girl who came tearing along the pavement on roller skates, nearly knocking him down on the way.

"Look at that. A girl on skates. Next they'll have boys with dolls," and he gave her a withering glance as she continued her reckless journey through the crowds.

An old man was blowing up balloons with a motor-tyre

pump and selling them a penny each. He was probably a roving balloon-man who went all over London, and his price was rather too high for Hoxton Street. They expect balloons for less than that, but perhaps he sold them cheaper later on. For the moment they were all passing him by.

Another old man with white hair was selling peppermints, half a pound for 3d. Yet the profit on these, such as it is, manages to keep him alive.

The toy-stalls in Hoxton Street are well worth seeing, and their prices even for new toys are quite a revelation. Few of them cost more than a few coppers each, and there is almost every kind of toy you can imagine.

For Pat, the day really began when he got to Burchall's stall. It also ended there, for by the time he had investigated all its contents there was no time left to do anything else.

It was kept by a father and two sons, and we were patiently entertained by Mr. Walter Burchall, one of the sons.

Pat immediately began roaming round the toys, and in a few seconds he had discovered a new form of pistol. He purchased it without hesitation, for his armoury did not include one of their kind. When I looked again, he was pointing it menacingly at the stall-holder. But Walter is shot many times a day and he did not turn a hair. When he is not too busy he will willingly throw up his hands or fall down dead.

I waited for an ear-splitting shot, but to my relief when Pat pulled the trigger the pistol only shone a light from a bulb at the end of the barrel. It had cost him 6d. all told.

"In summer, when cherries are in season," said Walter, "children bring us cherry-stones and ask if we'll take them in exchange for a doll. They think we use them for making the dolls' eyes."

"Do you sell sheath-knives?" interrupted Pat, jingling the remainder of his pocket-money.

"No," said Walter, and Pat's face fell.

"There are some twins," continued Walter, "about three

124

or four years old, who both have celluloid dolls which they bring to our dolls' hospital at the stall. If one breaks her doll's arm then the other one breaks her doll's arm too, and they both bring them in together. One day one of them stuck a pair of scissors into her doll's chest, so the other did the same thing."

"The battery will run down in a minute," I warned Pat, for he was busy looking at all the things by torchlight in spite of the clear daylight.

"It's a seven-hour battery," he informed me, and directed it into his mother's eye by way of a change.

"Some of them bring in dolls to be mended that we think are really not worth it," said Walter. "But they'd much rather spend a lot of money on having them repaired than pay much less for a brand-new one. Then some of them come in with an enormous great doll, saying they want a new one like it for twopence."

"Ping! Ping!" The sound of an eight-note piano rang across the shop.

Pat's mother was having a busy time frustrating all his attempts to start everything going. It was only her vigilance and presence of mind that saved the surrounding pavement from being overrun by the entire collection of clockwork motors, tanks, and animals. His fingers were itching to wind them up, and his heart ached to test their speed.

"You must have an endless amount of patience," I remarked to Walter.

"Oh, children come and spend the day here playing with things, and we can't tell 'em to go away. They come round barefoot in the summer when the men are cleaning the streets with hose-pipes. That's when they have a good paddle, and they splash plenty of mud on our toys as well as on themselves."

"Oh, boy, isn't it posh?" cried Pat, standing in front of a model fort. Many of his idioms flavour far more of Hollywood than they do of Ireland. He is an incorrigible film-goer,

125

and has an intelligent memory that holds every detail of all the films he sees.

Burchall's sell baby-chairs for 10s. 6d., and big teddy-bears for 5s. down to small ones for 6d. They have big dolls' houses for 3s. 6d. and toy shops for 1s. 11d. They even sell starch, macaroni, spaghetti, and ladies' hand-bags.

"How much are these d'oyleys?" a woman once asked Walter, referring to some obvious table-mats. "She was quite annoyed when we told her they weren't the thing to put on her dressing-table," he said.

Pat's mother and I were very footsore by the time we left the Burchalls' stall. But Pat himself was still as lively as when he started, and he went along flashing his gun into the doorways like a policeman. He was longing for nightfall more than words can say. Darkness with a pistol like that promised endless adventures.

There was little for him to flash it on inside the bus going home, so he amused himself by flashing it through his fingers and on his leg.

"Look at the hairs on my leg," he shouted, as if it was an epoch-making discovery.

"Hush!" said his mother, turning pink.

"I've got four on my chest," he announced shamelessly.

We were thankful to be sitting at the front of the bus, where the effect of this remark on the other passengers could not be seen.

"There's a master at our school," he told us, " who, when he's taking us for singing class, he tells us to sing from the top of our heads. And when he does that he tries to give a pull-up to his hair on the top of his forehead, but he's got none, so then he takes hold of a bit at the side."

This was not the first flashlight pistol he had. There had been others apparently, for he told us how he and his gang played a game at night called "Flash, flash, the Bogy Man."

"We were playing it once where they were building," he

said, his eyes glittering at the memory of it, "and we were right up on top of the scaffold poles. We led the night-watchman an awful dance an' all."

Pat is a delightful person, and he made our visit to Hoxton Street one of the happiest adventures I have had.

Chiswick

CHISWICK is one of the open street markets that have already been moved into a specially built closed arcade. It signifies more clearly than Rye Lane what will eventually happen to the street markets as we know them now. Also, while Rye Lane's arcade is only partially covered in, Chiswick is entirely covered, and is a comparatively modern building with a concrete floor and a conventional-looking entrance.

The most interesting thing about it is that it was first opened about eleven years ago, so the stall-holders have had a good chance to decide whether it is really an improvement. For them the plan has been a dreadful failure, and, as things are, it may not be long before the pretentious-looking market-place is vacated by all the stall-holders and has to be changed into something else.

At the far end of the market there are numbers of empty partitions, which look as though they have not seen a sign of life for some time. A few of the old stall-holders from the original open market still battle courageously against the odds of having a rent to pay and not being in the open pavement where people could not help seeing their wares.

Instead of only having to pay half a crown a week for a street-trading licence, they have to pay a rent that is far in excess of that amount. When people pass by an open street market they cannot help taking a peep at the goods, and then, times out of number, they are tempted to buy. They are attracted by the tumult of the street-cries and the excitement of the bidding. And they know that a street market is likely to be cheap. But when they pass a covered building, that has stall partitions almost like shops, they are not drawn to go inside. Probably they surmise that it is no cheaper than the shops, though in actual fact the old stall-holders do try to keep to their street-market prices.

129

Those who remain in this market are clustered as near as possible to the entrance, in a pathetic effort to be seen by the Chiswick shoppers. The final note of irony in their fate, is that the two outside places at the opening of the market are occupied by a flourishing modern cut-price grocery stores. Their wares are piled round the entrance, so that some of them half bulge outside and cannot fail to attract attention. The real old stall-holders of the street market have to take a back seat just behind them.

This is what the old stall-holders have to put up with, and already some of them have been crushed by a system which is designed to improve. Unless some way can be found of making provision for the street-traders to trade under cover without crippling their trade, the future years will see the end of them. We shall not only miss the picturesque old rickety stalls and the advantage of their bargains, but we shall lose the varied, and many of them lovable, characters who have made these bargains possible.

It was Saturday when I went there, the busiest day for all the household street markets, but Chiswick Market was strangely quiet.

Mrs. Hawkins buys and sells second-hand clothes at the far end near all those empty partitions, and I think they rather haunt her.

"What about the green coat?" asked a young woman, who was evidently trying to make some pocket-money out of a cast-off garment that Mrs. Hawkins was trying to sell for her on commission.

"Still there," said Mrs. Hawkins laconically. "Are you leavin' it or takin' it?"

"I'll leave it," said the girl half-heartedly. "Will you be here next week?"

"Hope so, if they don't turn us out. They're nearly all gone except me." Mrs. Hawkins looked dismally at the empty partitions.

She told me she used to be in the old open street market.

130

"It's the rents that's so dear," she explained sadly. "A pound a week for three brick walls like these!" She glanced at them as though she would very much like to set fire to them.

"When do you do most business?" But it was a sore question to have asked.

"Mainly Saturdays we do a bit. That's all. I've stood here the whole week and only took five shillings. It was all right in the old days when we was outside. We didn't have all this expense and we did have a bit of trade. Can't think why they ever moved us in here," she said bitterly.

Mr. Izzard is a lovable old person who keeps a stall of tempting fresh bacon, eggs, butter, and lard. He told me he had spent eleven years inside the new market and he had a stall in the old street market for eight years before that.

"Do you like being in here best?" I asked, hoping to find a different opinion.

"No; outside best," he said, without hesitation. "We used to get the people then. The stalls were just near here, you know, outside the 'Prince of Wales.' "

Mr. Izzard still hangs on, keeping his prices almost as reasonable as they were in the open street-market days.

"I still have many of me old customers who stay by me," he explained.

He is the kind of stall-holder who would have faithful, devoted old customers. And he deserves them.

Mr. Izzard's bacon costs from 3½d. to 1s. a pound, and hocks are 4½d. to 6d. Eggs go from sixteen a shilling. He is a dependable person and his bacon is very good.

"I do nearly all my business on Saturday nights, just for about two hours, and for about an hour Friday night. Before I took to the old street market I used to have three provision shops. But things is altered since then. We're growing old, you know," he said philosophically.

I think if I had gone to that market on any other day in the week, I should have found them all asleep from sheer

131

lack of customers. Even on Saturday they were very subdued, as though their troubles oppressed them.

Miss Huxley is another character who used to be in the original market. She sells salads, vegetables, and flowers, besides the "cooked beets" which are such a popular feature of the street markets. There is almost a charm about cooking beetroots successfully, and that is why so many housewives much prefer to buy them ready cooked. If they are tackled by an unskilled hand they are apt to "bleed," and then they appear pale and anæmic looking, without any flavour, and the term "as red as a beetroot" becomes distressingly inapt.

When I asked her where she liked being best, she said, "Outside, of course," very abruptly. Again I had turned the knife in the wound.

"Can I 'ave 'em back by to-night? They're all she's got," pleaded a woman who had brought in her little girl's shoes to Fillips, the cobbler.

"I doubt if I can let you have them to-day. I've got a terrible lot to do," said Mr. Fillips.

Then he looked down at the little girl's feet, which were covered with a pair of old canvas shoes that had let in the wet.

"If you look in this evening I'll do my very best for you," he said. And when the woman had gone he shook his head sadly at the little shoes, which were almost past repairing.

Mr. Fillips does all the cobbling alone. He charges only 2s. 6d. for "ladies', sole an' heel" instead of the usual 4s. 6d. "Heels only" are "6d. and 9d. ladies'" instead of 1s., and men's, 1s. 3d. He cobbles about thirty pairs of shoes a day.

But this cobbler is not the original one who was in the open street market, and this chapter is really for the real old street-traders.

Mrs. Wakeman was a very popular person in the open-air days, and she still has a great many "faithfuls" among her customers. She has a big fruit and vegetable stall which she presides over herself, and the other side of the market she also has a flower-stall which somebody else keeps an eye on for her.

132

She was serving when I went to see her, and had quite a little cluster of customers round her.

"What sort yer like, dear?" she asked a woman who wanted apples. "Two bunches rhubard, twopence," she said to the next customer, pushing the rhubarb into her shopping-bag.

"I've bin with me stall twenty years," she told me. "I was nine years outdoors. In some ways I don't mind whether I'm in or out, duck, but the worst thing here is it's so expensive. Of course the trouble outside was that they hadn't got no control like they have in the street markets now. Everybody used to come on it, and the market was pretty big. Folk could crowd in with their stall how they liked.

"Now it's so expensive there's only a few of us can keep on. So many of the places are empty in here now because of what it costs. Some say it's going to sell out and some say not. Oh, I don't know what's going to be. I wonder what'll happen," she said thoughtfully, as she turned her head and glanced anxiously at all the empty partitions.

I wonder too.

Ridley Road

STREET-TRADERS are subject to laws and discipline just as much as any other citizens. They have to pay a licence fee of half a crown a week, for which they are also granted a certificate for the current year by their local borough council. There are strict regulations as to the size and shape of their stalls and the distance between them. And the official allocations must not be tampered with in any way. Albeit there are bandits who try to elude these laws, and so there has to be some one to watch over them and "go the round" of the stalls every day.

The street-market inspectors are the guardian angels of all the stall-holders. They are also very strict disciplinarians where licences are out of date. I met one of the nicest of them in Ridley Road, and followed him on his round.

To people living in West London or many of the suburbs, Ridley Road is quite a fair distance. It means taking a long and irksome journey by bus to Church Street, Stoke Newington, and then going by tram into Hackney. The same tram sets you down at Ridley Road. But even the tedious journey is worth it, for Ridley Road is one of the largest street markets and full of life and bustle. There are plenty of bargains, besides a good variety of wares, and it has a great deal of spontaneous entertainment.

When I arrived at Ridley Road, I saw a tall, erect figure in uniform and a peaked cap standing in the middle of the road talking to a policeman. He had a fresh, open-air face, a kind smile, charming manners, and, as I learned later, a very sympathetic understanding of all human nature. And that was my street-market inspector.

He took me round the market while he finished his duties, and in between he told me scraps about its life and ways.

135

"There are about two hundred stalls in the market," he said, as we wound our way through the crowds and zig-zagged round the stalls. "Thursdays and Saturdays are the two best days. Most of the stall-holders are licensed for the whole week, but some of them are only licensed for certain days."

I asked him about the famous old characters in the market.

"There are one or two old-time costers," he told me, "but I'll show you those later on.

"Some of them put up a board with their name painted on it. But we always issue a card, which they have to be ready to produce whenever we ask them for it. The cards are a different colour each year. Then the stalls have to be either nine feet, six feet, or five feet in length and so on. There has to be a three-foot gangway between each stall." And he showed me the painted boundaries on the kerb.

Suddenly his alert eyes lighted on an expired card hanging on a little stall which did not seem to be doing much trade.

"That's nineteen-thirty-five," he said, tapping it with his finger, and looking sternly at the stall-holder.

"Yes," said the man, shifting nervously from one foot to the other, while his eyes ran from side to side as he tried to think of an excuse.

"It ought to be nineteen-thirty-six. Why haven't you got it yet?"

The man's eyes ran round faster than ever.

"The wife hasn't been able to get round for it yet. She's been ill. But she's hoping to be up Monday and she'll get round then," he added hastily. He spoke rather thickly through a large mouthful of bread and cheese which he was eating when we arrived.

"Are you here all the week?"

"Yes."

"I'll see it on Tuesday," said the inspector firmly, but not unkindly. And the stall-holder almost choked with relief.

A moment later we were crossing the road, and the in-

136

spector nodded towards a stall on wheels that was piled high with bananas.

"That man with the bananas is not a licensed man. You'll see him begin to move away directly he sees me."

And sure enough the next minute the man looked up in the middle of serving a customer, and in another second he was wheeling his stall on as fast as he could. He did not run away, but wheeled it towards us and faced the music. Perhaps that was why the inspector was not so sharp with him as I expected.

"You've no right to be here," he called out sternly. "Get away quickly."

"Yes—I'm going, sir," the lad answered him with a smile that was not impertinent.

"We try to allocate the stalls as far as possible to separate the different trades. For instance, we don't put a butcher's stall exactly outside a butcher's shop or next door to another butcher's stall. That stall just beside us happens to sell the same things as the shop, because it really belongs to the people who keep the shop."

Then the inspector went up to an old man with a green-grocer's stall that was surrounded by stale cabbage-leaves and bits of paper.

"Is your son back, Ted?" he asked peremptorily, but kindly.

"Yes, he's there, and he's just going to clear away all the rubbish. Otherwise he's for it."

And Ted made an expressive gesture to show what would happen to his son's posterior if he failed to obey orders. Evidently the inspector had discovered the untidy pavement earlier in the morning, and been told by Ted that his son was going to clear it up, but had dashed off on an urgent errand first.

Then we met an old woman who sells medicines which she brews herself over the kitchen fire. Each mixture is attended by the name of some illness, and I was rash enough

137

to stop and admire her array. Immediately she began talking to me and crooning over me, as though I was going through the last stages of some fatal disease.

"What is it you be wantin', dear?" she asked. And she began telling me all she could do for me. Then she edged nearer to me and put her arm round me. But the inspector's tall figure interposed and I managed to escape, nodding and smiling to humour her as I left.

"She comes out in white riding-breeches sometimes," said the inspector, when we were farther away.

Apparently she is the butt of Ridley Road, and the stall-holders all play jokes on her. If she gets annoyed with them she thinks nothing of throwing a bucket of water over them, and she has a flow of language that would shake almost any one.

The other stall-holders tell how, when the nation was in mourning for the late King, she turned up dressed in black from head to foot, and they told her she was being very disloyal in not wearing a veil. Next day she turned up in a tremendous long black veil that hung all the way down in front of her and right down her back as well.

Another time one of them proposed to her in the market for a joke, and asked her to meet him at Westminster Abbey the next Monday afternoon. Monday came and the old woman arrived at Westminster Abbey, only to find her mock suitor was nowhere to be seen. So she went into the Abbey and gave the vergers a distinctly trying half-hour, while she plagued them to know where he was and accused them of sending him off. Then when she got back to the street market next day, she chased the unfortunate stall-holder all down the street with a heavy stick.

Her chief off-duty occupation consists of visiting the police-station and making voluble complaints about her fellow-stall-holders. The police are getting quite accustomed to her now and they find that, with a little tactful humouring, she goes away.

138

"You see that man over there, standing in the road smoking a cigar?" said the inspector; "he's an ex-convict."

I looked at what I should have mistaken for a highly prosperous business-man, and decided he was a good recommendation for prison life.

Later on the inspector commented on him too. "It's a funny thing about that man," he said. "He's like so many of them, wonderfully philosophic about it all and sees the funny side. He's ready for anything—pickpocketing, burglaries, anything he can find to do. Yet to meet, he's a most amusing, charming person with a real sense of humour." Then he introduced me to one of the nicest people in Ridley Road.

"This is Barnard, our old soldier," he said.

"Yes," said the old man proudly, "I'm the only Old Contemptible in the market."

He had a clean, tidy stall and a highly polished old ship's bell hanging in the centre of it. His was a curious occupation for a man, but one gets used to surprises in a street market. "Corsets made to measure," said the notice displayed over a quantity of pink elastic underwear.

A man called Burgess has a very good bacon-stall. And there is a stall there that sells nothing but pickles. But there are many other wares besides food on the stalls in Ridley Road, including new and old clothes and all kinds of useful things for the house.

"How old do you think old Mother Levy is?" asked the inspector, when we came up to an old man selling vegetables.

"About eighty," said the man. "I'm seventy-six and me father's still doin' things and reads without glasses."

I looked across the road at old Mother Levy, who was sitting perched on her chair behind her greengrocery-stall. She was wrapped up in quantities of woollies, with a leather motoring-coat on top of them. And she was so silent and still that it was just as if some wicked fairy had come and turned her to stone.

139

Later on, over a cup of coffee in his lunch-hour, the inspector told me many interesting things about the inside life of this street market. He warned me first that he could not tell me any official secrets of the Council. But I assured him that I was not seeking for them.

" When the stall-holders think one of the inspectors is on the watch they warn each other, saying, 'So-and-so's on the coat and badge.' Then they say 'under the cain and abel' when they mean underneath the stall. They call their girl-friends their 'donahs,' and a summons is 'a blister.'

"There's a man who has a fruit-stall in Ridley Road who had a glass of water beside him when he was selling one night. 'Look what we trade on! Water!' he called out, and then he drank it down in front of the crowd. But he'd had eleven pints of beer between twelve in the morning and ten o'clock that night, so I think that glass of water must have cost him something in courage to drink it down like that!"

He told me how, although many of them were uneducated and illiterate to the last degree, most of the street-traders had a wonderful sense of intuition. They knew instinctively whether they could take a person in or not, and whether they were in any danger of being caught out breaking laws.

"If you're an inspector you've got to be top-dog," he said, "and as long as you let them know without being too harsh over it, they will give remarkably little trouble."

But this inspector's duties did not end in Ridley Road.

"There are just under a thousand stalls in Hackney," he told me. "There are seven street markets in the borough, and I go round four of them—Ridley Road, Broadway London Fields, Garnham Street, and Kingsland Waste. The others are Chatsworth Road, Well Street, and Hackney Wick.

"Kingsland Waste is a Saturdays-only street market. They sell spare parts of bicycles, tap-washers, and wireless parts, besides a certain amount of glassware, clothing, lengths of material, not to mention second-hand cricket-bats and tennis-

140

racquets. But the main features are wireless parts and bicycle parts. Men go there after work on Saturday afternoon and hunt round for bits and pieces to mend or improve their wireless sets or bicycles. Then they spend the week-end fitting them on."

The inspector told me a very romantic story about a stall-holder in Kingsland Waste.

"He used to be a clerk of the better type, earning about two hundred and fifty pounds a year. He's a very nice fellow, but he got the sack in a year when every one was cutting down their staff. By the time he had tried hard to get in anywhere he was literally penniless. He came to us to ask if it would be possible for him to procure a street-trading licence, and he offered us seven wireless parts in exchange for it—all he had. We gave him the licence, and he managed to set up selling wireless parts in Kingsland Waste. Now he's really doing quite well, averaging about four pounds a week he told me.

"Most of Ridley Road Street Market has only been going about nine or ten years," the inspector went on, "but some of the stalls at the top have been there much longer. In the old days, before we had the present system, there were about twenty positions allocated. All the street-traders used to be up by about four in the morning, waiting in the side-streets. Then when it was the usual opening-time, the policeman used to blow his whistle, and they'd run fighting and screaming to try and get the positions. After that all the unlucky ones had to go away and come again the next day."

Apparently there used to be a man with some performing white mice in Ridley Road, but he had been away some weeks when I was there. He was an Italian, and he had a long rod with a bell at one end, and the mice used to run up the rod and ring the bell with their tiny paws.

"The food-stalls always have to give the address of their storage, so that it can be inspected. But we don't do that. There are special men for that job," said the inspector.

141

"Many of the street-traders buy what they call 'seconds and thirds'—cheap quality goods from the warehouses. Then they let them go cheap and quickly, which they call 'knocking out a cochell.' Then unlicensed men often pay scouts to watch out for them."

I asked him if the inspectors had to settle disputes in the street market. "The traders sometimes have rows with a customer over change," he said, "but we try and refrain from interfering in any way with the actual trading in the market. Of course, if there's any real trouble and somebody starts a brawl, the police deal with it. We sometimes find one stall-holder telling another that he's not selling a real medicine, it's only sugar and water—and all that kind of thing."

A street-market inspector does not have an easy job, but this one thoroughly enjoyed it.

"I wouldn't have another job for anything in the world," he said sincerely; "even if I was to have a lot more money for something else, I wouldn't change." (I could think of many jobs where his tact and sympathy would have been invaluable.) "That's one thing. Then look how healthy it is being out in the open air. I was badly underweight when I started not long ago, and now I'm just about right."

He made me laugh by describing how, on wet days, the stall-holders have big tarpaulins over their stalls, which collect large puddles of rain-water. Then, when it's fine again, they will suddenly throw them back without looking what they are doing, just as somebody is walking past. And the unhappy person gets a pretty heavy drenching.

When we were going along the Hoxton High Street again, we ran into the man with the unlicensed banana-stall. He had been selling more bananas on the way, so his flight had not been a swift one.

"How many times have you been in prison, Howard?" asked the inspector.

The young man smiled cheerfully as he touched his forehead.

142

"Very nearly a hundred, sir," he said with another broad smile.

"Yes, I should think it must be just about that number," said the inspector dryly. "You'd better be careful or you'll be having another little holiday at the King's expense," he said, but not too harshly. And the lad touched his forehead again and hurried away.

That was what I admired about the inspector. His discipline was very firm, but his severity was tempered with kindness and sympathy and was far more effective in consequence. He understood the difficulties those people had to face. And they knew he understood, so they gave him very little trouble. Even the lad he had sent to prison so often, obviously looked on him as a friend. Probably the lawbreakers like him best, because they experience his kindness more often and in cases where it is most needed though less deserved.

The inspector is one of the greatest people I have ever met. But he will not let me give away his name.

Kingston-on-Thames

THERE are very interesting street markets and open-air markets in some of London's suburbs. The one at Kingston-on-Thames is probably the oldest and best known of them. It has an old charter granted them in the reign of King Charles in the year 1629, giving them a right to hold the market without allowing any other market to set up within seven miles of it.

The older generation of stall-holders have nearly all disappeared from this market, and youth has taken their place. But it is **a** very thriving market, and the stalls are piled lavishly with appetising food and good produce. Most of the people seem cheerful and prosperous, and there is certainly no lack of trade at any time, though Saturday is the busiest day of all.

I stopped by a large greengrocery-stall, which was presided over by a very rural-looking individual with carroty hair, and a small boy who seemed to be the life and soul of the vicinity.

"They call me 'Titch,' " said the boy when I asked him his name. He does the calling out on Saturday night in a high, piping voice.

"Best kidney taters, five pounds for a tanner," he calls; "lovely ripe bananas."

"Some folks come with a very big bag and ask for 'alf a pound of sprouts," he told me. "Then when we've weighed 'em out they say, 'Would you mind putting me another one in, in case one's bad?' "

Mrs. Vince has had her fish-stall in Kingston for seventeen years, and she has a tremendous array of very good fish, not to speak of cockles and whelks. She is quiet and not informative, but I noticed she had a following of aristocratic and well-to-do customers.

If you want to buy really healthy, well-kept pets at market prices, you should go and see Thomas Ling. He has luxurious-looking Angora rabbits, several kinds of pigeons, puppies, and hens. Mr. Ling is only there on Saturdays, for he also goes to Guildford and Basingstoke. But he is a Kingston man, and he lives and breeds his pets at Kingston.

I missed seeing him because he was away at lunch. But Mr. Lilley, who has the next stall, said, "I stood next him for thirty years. I might be able to enlighten you." But beyond these short scraps of information it turned out that he was too busy to tell me more.

Young Mr. Wilnot calls himself the "nut merchant." Like old Poulteney of the Shepherd's Bush Street Market, he does an enormous trade in them. He is there on Thursday, Friday, and Saturday, and his prices are very fair—chestnuts 4d. a pound, and brazils 6d. a pound.

"There's a great many folk who come every week and eat nuts like you would sweets. When they ask for a pound 'a mixed nuts they say, 'Don't put any coco-nuts in among 'em.' That's *their* chestnut all right, I can tell you!"

I bought some tulips from a man with a little flower-stall, who said he had three acres of ground at Molesley where he grew all his flowers.

"I'm here every day in the week," he said, "except Sundays and Mondays, when I do a bit of digging."

Everybody in Kingston Market wanted to tell me about the old man who goes round Kingston wearing the most extraordinary clothes he can find, and hires himself out as a sandwich-man to advertise local galas or somebody's boats on the river.

But he is nothing to do with the market, though he appears to be the talk of the town, and you will always find the talk of the town in the market.

Having been established for fifty years, Hillyers deems it necessary to have a board with "ye olde winkle-stall" painted on it. You can go and have a dainty morsel of any kind of

146

small shell-fish there for 1½d. a plate. Cockles, mussels, whelks, and so on. There they are, all laid out waiting for you to be tempted by them.

"It's my father's stall," said the little girl who was looking after it. "It used to be my granddad's, but you see he's dead."

Nearby is Mrs. Wilson's tea-stall, where she doles out cups of tea with a motherly air to all the shivering customers and stall-holders on a winter's day.

" 'Elp yerself to a tea-cake, duck," she adds. And she generally has to go to the cut-price stall next door to get some change.

At one corner of the market there is a stall which is just as though a bit of the Caledonian Market had strayed into Kingston. It is a stall of second-hand silver, jewellery, and silver antiques.

Just like the Caledonian silver kings, he is strangely secretive about his wares, and I think he would like to wear a mask and have a screen around his stall. All the same, his stall is worth keeping an eye on, for it often has interesting "finds" for a collector.

The chief features of Kingston open market are fish and fruit, followed by vegetables, plants, and flowers. It is always a riot of gay colours and tempting goods. And it has a country flavour and an air of happy prosperity that does one good.

A Peep into the Past

IF we went to look for New Cut and Lower Marsh in the sixteenth century, we should have found only a vast, swampy trait of uninhabited marshland.

Lambeth Marsh was the name given to the whole of this swampy ground which stretched along the Thames between Lambeth Church and Blackfriars. And Lower Marsh, as we know it now, was then part of it.

The nineteenth century saw the marsh cultivated, and it became open fields. Cottages, sheds, and tea-gardens sprang up, and soon the countryside disappeared and was covered instead with a network of narrow streets and mean houses.

The district to-day has an atmosphere of brooding evil, and it is interesting to find that this was no mere fancy on my part. It is recorded in a history of London that "The more inhabited parts were notorious as the haunts of thieves, prostitutes, and sharpers" in the early nineteenth century, and it has kept that character all along.

Very little is recorded of the earliest of London's street markets, though we can get an idea of their position in the nineteenth century from Wheatley and Cunningham, who published a volume on *London, Past and Present* in 1891.

They give an extract from an article by Henry Mayhew, which appeared in a paper called the *Morning Chronicle* in 1849.

Mayhew tells us "of these street markets there are fifteen held throughout London every Saturday night and Sunday morning."

Nowadays there are over a hundred street markets in London, functioning either the whole of the week or on certain days.

Evidently in Mayhew's day most of the hucksters in the

fifteen centred round New Cut. "The most crowded of these are held in that part of Lambeth called the New Cut, and in that part of Somers Town known as 'The Brill.' These are both about half a mile in length, and each of them is frequented by as nearly as possible three hundred hucksters."

He describes the hucksters as "a dense line of itinerant tradesmen." So evidently they wandered at will on the days when they did not stand in the market.

Apparently the wares they sold were much the same thing as they offer to-day, except for "silk and straw bonnets, nightcaps, tea-kettles, and Dutch ovens."

There were no street-trading licences, and according to Mayhew the hucksters were free agents to sell where they pleased.

"These street markets are perfectly free, anybody being at liberty to stand with his goods, and the 'pitch' or stand being secured simply by letting the wares down upon the most desirable spot that might be vacant. In order to select this, the hucksters usually arrive at the market at four o'clock in the afternoon, and having chosen their 'pitch' they leave the articles they have for sale in the custody of a boy, until six o'clock, when the market begins.

"The class of customers in these places are mostly the wives of mechanics and labourers. . . . After pay-time on Saturday night or on Sunday morning the crowd in New Cut and the Brill in particular, is almost impassable. Indeed the scene in these parts has more of the character of a fair than a market.

"There are hundreds of stalls, and every stall has its light. Either it is illuminated by the bright white light of the new self-generating gas lamp, or else it is lighted by the red smoky flare of the old-fashioned grease lamp."

From Mayhew's description of the street-cries they were very much like the street-cries of to-day, except for ones like "Who'll buy a bonnet for fourpence?"

"Such indeed is the riot and struggle," wrote Mayhew,

150

"and the scramble for a living that, wild as the scene of the London Docks appeared, the confusion and uproar of the New Cut on Saturday night overwhelms the thoughtful mind."

To us this account sounds much more like Petticoat Lane, for New Cut as we know it now has gone down considerably since then. We have to look in other parts of London now to find the liveliest street markets that present a picture like Mayhew found at New Cut.

He tells how, in those times, the same scene took place in the Brill, Leather Lane, Tottenham Court Road, and Whitecross Street.

"Go to whatever corner of the Metropolis you please, either on Saturday night or on a Sunday morning, and there is the same shouting to get the penny profit out of the poor man's dinner."

Tottenham Court Road no longer has a street market, and the Brill has passed out of existence, but Leather Lane and Whitecross Street are still flourishing street markets.

After quoting from Mayhew's article, Wheatley and Cunningham tell us: "More than thirty years have passed and the scene is not materially changed. There is some change in the articles offered, and in the character of the stalls and stall-keepers, but the crowd, the glare and the noise and confusion continue, though there is perhaps somewhat less tumult.

"The Brill has been swept away by the Midland Railway Company, but the hucksters have taken possession of the neighbouring streets."

The second-hand magazine-stalls which are to be found in so many of the street markets, existed even in those times. It is recorded that in Whitechapel and Shoreditch "the literary tastes of the East End folk are provided for by brightly lighted stalls of second-hand books, the supply being largely composed of religious works, old magazines, and cheap illustrated volumes." But the magazines were probably mainly ones that have passed out of existence now, and a good many of them would be religious tracts.

New Cut must only have completed its change of face from country to town early in the nineteenth century. There is an account of a mob assembling in 1815 "to pull down a windmill in the belief that, as the lease had run out, the material of the building had become common property."

We are told by Stow, a famous historian of the sixteenth century, that Leather Lane used to be known as Lither Lane, "a turning also to the field, late replenished with houses built and so to the bar."

He gives a long list of old inns, some of which are still there now, though probably partly restored. From his description of Leather Lane it has evidently improved a good deal since he wrote about it.

"The lane traverses a very poor neighbourhood," he relates in speaking of it then, "is infested with thieves and beggars, and is in itself narrow and dirty, lined with stalls and barrows and itinerant dealers in fish, bacon, vegetables, plasterers' or image shops, and old clothes."

Leather Lane is still narrow and it is still a street market, but its character is much more attractive than in those days.

Petticoat Lane is the kind of street market that makes us long to dip into its past. Apparently it was formerly called Hog Lane, and again it is to Stow that we owe an account of its beginning.

"In ancient times, on both sides of this lane were hedgerows and elm trees, with pleasant fields to walk in. Insomuch that some gentlemen of the Court and City built their houses here for air."

When Stow was a boy, a Spanish ambassador in the reign of King James I. had his house built there and lived there for some time. The King's jeweller had "a fair and large house" there too. Many of the French Protestants who fled to England in the reign of James I. came to live in Petticoat Lane, and followed their trade, which was weaving.

152

Wheatley and Cunningham tell us that, "as the weavers receded from Petticoat Lane it was occupied by Jews. And for a long series of years its inhabitants have been Jews of the least respectable class, and the houses and shops receptacles for second-hand clothes and stolen goods. On Sunday morning it is noisy and crowded with clamorous buyers and sellers of old jewellery and old clothes and old wares of all kinds."

In other words, very much the same Petticoat Lane we know to-day.

Before Farringdon Street Street Market came into being there was the old Farringdon Market between Farringdon Street and Shoe Lane, "established for the sale of fruit and vegetables, and for the removal of Fleet Street markets for the present Farringdon Street. The west side of the market was swept away in forming the approaches to the Holborn Viaduct. The remainder looks neglected and dilapidated.

"Farringdon Street extends from Bridge Street, Blackfriars, to the Farringdon Road at the crossing of Holborn Viaduct. The centre was formerly occupied by Fleet Market, and on the east side stood the Fleet Prison (pulled down in 1846). Fleet Ditch, once a river and now a sewer, runs beneath the centre of the street."

"Islington was renowned for beggars and thieves." It was "the first halting-place for London on the Great North Road, and was a favourite place for the pursuit of their calling."

Very little information is to be found of the earlier days of the street markets, though there are many interesting scraps of history about the streets that are now famous for their street markets.

In 1708 Berwick Street was "a kind of a Row. The fronts of the houses resting on columns made a small piazza," which suggests to us that even then it was an Italian quarter. "George Anne Bellamy, the famous actress, lived in this street when she was in pecuniary distress."

Bethnal Green is described by Wheatley and Cunningham as being "one of the chief quarters of the costermongers of London." So the present street markets in the district must have been formed from when these costermongers gathered together in chosen streets to sell their wares as noisily as possible.

There is a reference which intimates the existence of part of Berwick Street Market in their account of Little Poulteney Street. Apparently it used to be called the "Knaves Acre." Then a Mr. Poultney of St. James's became "the owner of certain messuages and tenements in a certain place called Soho" as early as 1645. It is supposed that Poulteney Street was called after him.

A description of Knaves Acre in 1720 says that it was "but narrow and chiefly inhabited by those that deal in old goods and glass bottles," which may be taken to have meant the beginning of the hucksters in that part.

Shoreditch has Hoxton Street as the most famous street market in the borough. It is interesting to learn that the mock title "Duke of Shoreditch" used to be bestowed on "the most successful archer in the annual trials of skill." The title was first used in the reign of Henry VIII.

As soon as the hucksters began putting up stalls instead of just spreading their goods on the pavements, they became subject to rules about the size of these stalls which vary very slightly from the present time.

In the Liber Albus of London these rules were referred to under the old laws about "The Cleansing of the Streets and Lanes of the City."

One rule decrees that "no stall shall be more than two feet and a half in breadth, and that it shall be moveable and flexible."

Another law stated that "no stall be beyond the house of a greater breadth than two feet, or at the discretion of the Aldermen according as the streets or lanes are broad or narrow."

154

Introducing the Caledonian Market

HERE is the happy hunting-ground of hundreds of roving cheap-jacks, and the largest and most popular of all the London street markets.

One of the joys it has for the cheap-jacks is that it is a toll-market. Instead of paying for a licence each week, they only pay a small toll at the gate whenever they go in. Some of the dishonest ones try to evade the toll by turning up with a friend, and hiding their wares in a suit-case. Then one of them goes in through the gate as an ordinary member of the public, who do not have to pay, and he gets his friend to throw the suit-case over the railings.

The market is a mile square, and crammed with hucksters selling all manner of different wares. You have to ride patiently up the long, dreary Caledonian Road, then take a turning to the left at the far end, and go up a short hill which is crowned by the market.

You will see it enclosed in thick iron railings, and it has a clock-tower, besides a covered part in the centre. But all the rest is a wide-open concrete space, with railings and divisions. There, before your eyes, the millions of wares are spread like a kind of magic carpet, some on stalls and many on the ground. All kinds of quaint characters come and earn a living there, and people from every walk of life wander through the market looking for some precious "find."

Tuesday and Friday are the only two days when the market is open as a street market—Friday being the busier day of the two. On other week-days it is used as a cattle-market and the cheap-jacks are excluded from it.

Most of the cheap-jacks are there regularly all the year round. Some of them only appear once, sell a quantity of valuable things, and disappear. Maybe if a customer has to

155

go back and complain of anything, they will find the stall-holder gone. You have to be very astute over shopping in the Caledonian Market, though there are plenty of honest stall-holders who have quite a happy reputation.

Apart from your own personal discomfort it is best to choose a fine day, because so many of the stall-holders stay away in wet weather. Their goods lie unprotected on the ground, so they could not risk having them ruined by a deluge of rain. That is why their spirits are highest during a long fine spell. But even then they will turn anxious eyes to watch a passing cloud, in case it is a warning that they should begin to pack up and take flight.

The Caledonian is a pageant of queer things and strange people. Probably more valuable antiques have been "picked up for a song" there than anywhere else. There is all the excitement of never knowing what you are going to see next. And for the real bargain-hunters it has a glamorous spell that draws them back to it again and again.

But come through those great iron gates and see for yourself.

The Junk Merchants

THE junk merchants have claimed a large part of the Caledonian Market, and their wares present the strangest
accumulation of things you can imagine.

They have no stalls, but spread them out on the ground,
and it is difficult to know where one cheap-jack's things end
and another's begin. I wondered whether they sometimes
quarrel over the ownership of some old bits and pieces that
have got muddled up, but they all seem to get along quite
amicably, in spite of the nearness of their rivals.

When I walked past Mr. H. Judd's pitch I saw some old
rag-dolls heaped among cast-off paint-brushes, footballs,
tennis-balls (looking extremely weather-beaten), and all kinds
of bits of broken indoor games. There were odd rubber
heels resting on an old tennis-racquet, not to speak of an
impossible-looking chair and quite a presentable dustbin.
He had rolls of wallpaper too, but you would probably have
had to make the walls like a patchwork quilt, for the rolls
were small and unalike.

He was very secretive about where he found his junk.
"Oh, I jus' goes huntin' all the week," he said. And I wondered if he was afraid I was thinking of starting a junk-stall
of my own.

"Any price yer like," invited a woman selling pots of
paint and varnishes.

"Do you come and paint the house as well?" I asked

"Na," she said scornfully. "They buy a can of paint and
do it theirselves."

But our conversation was cut short by a car with a horn
that blew "cuckoo" at me and nearly ran me down.

Many of the more prosperous stall-holders have cars in
the Caledonian, and use them for carrying their wares to the

market. There is a big parking-place outside, which is always packed with cars while the traders hold court inside the market.

I stopped by a piece of ground that was smothered in a confusion of locks, keys, bolts, and disused carpenters' saws and braces. It seemed deserted.

"Whose stall is this?" I asked a man who was brushing up some old bowler hats.

"The gentleman of the next department. That's him, standing there on the cobbles," he said in his best shop-walker's manner, waving his brush in the direction of a young man who was having a gossip nearby. But at this moment the man saw somebody was taking an interest in his stall and hurried over to see what was happening.

"Locks and files, twopence a piece. Any offers?" he called, rubbing his hands. "Come 'ere if you want to buy the stuff. Come 'ere. Saws a shilling."

But I changed my mind about talking to him.

"Lady, lend me a pound before yer go away, will yer, please?" he shouted derisively at my back.

A man called Martin told me he collected all his junk from Hampstead and Kingston. He probably does it in a car and carries on some other trade as well. He had twenty-four brass stair-rods for 6s. or less. "They got wet in the rain this morning," he explained. He also had a slop-pail filled with embroidery silks, and a medley of grubby Venetian blinds, old books, and old mangles.

I heard a woman call out to another junk merchant, "I'll buy that pram if you'll send it home for me."

"Oh yes," he replied sarcastically. "I'll come round and roll the bloomin' kid out for you Sunday morning, if you like. Did you ever hear anything like it in your life—an' all for half a crown!"

Judging by the look of the pram I should have said it would have dropped to bits directly anybody tried to wheel it along. But perhaps he managed to get the half-crown from some one before they moved it.

158

One pitch just had a radio-set with a pair of old shoes on top. But I did not have a chance to go back and see whether the poor old man had sold either the radio-set or the pair of old shoes.

There were plenty of old radio-sets. A cheap-jack called Brown had a three-valve set that worked beautifully, going for 15s., and he may have knocked it down later in the day. He also had a large solid mahogany dressing-table mirror on a stand, really quite unharmed, for 7s. 6d.

I did find a large cabinet H.M.V. gramophone being sold for 25s., though it was certainly not an up-to-date model. The man who had it makes a speciality of mainsprings for gramophones, which he sells off cheaply.

The old-clothes women have their pitches mingled among the junk merchants. A few of them are rather grand and have improvised stalls, but most of them pile their clothes on the pavement or on strips of newspaper. The conversations that go on round them are often very amusing, if you can bear being in such close proximity to some of the old clothes.

I saw one woman pick up a vivid purple-and-pink striped undergarment.

"Would those fit you?" asked the old-clothes woman hopefully.

But the other one went off into derisive shrieks of laughter. "No, my old man wouldn't 'alf go off if he saw me putting them on," she said, churning the pile of clothes with her hands to see what else she could find.

Many of them take their friends and go and rout among all the old clothes, just to see what they can find to joke about. Then they go away feeling immensely fashionable in comparison.

Sometimes you can find quite valuable bits of old furniture in the junk-stalls. Most of the chairs are sold for 1s. to 4s. each, and the tables for 5s. And I saw one of the old men with chairs in his junk, selling a large coffee-grinder for 6d.

And it worked—or at least the handle went round, for he was turning it.

The Caledonian has its nearest approach to a motor-car merchant in Blower's pavement collection of second-hand spare parts.

"We can sell you a complete car—in parts," he added with a sober twinkle.

I looked down at a terrific array of motor-car mirrors, speedometers, head-lamps, steering-wheels, and anything that could be found to go on a car. There was even a whole engine waiting to be bought.

On days when he is not in the market, Blower is a car-breaker, and from buying up old cars and reselling their component parts as "spares," he is able to make a reasonable living.

Nearby there were bedsteads with quite good springs for 5s. 6d. They had obviously been re-painted and were then an arresting, if unpleasantly vivid bright blue colour.

"No—not there," murmured a quiet intellectual man, who was looking through a pile of old copies of music that were lying on the ground.

"What are you looking for?" I asked.

"Just some Grieg I haven't got."

He told me he was a pianist, and that he bought nearly all his classical music in the Caledonian Market. Apparently he went there very often, and had a hunt round for any particular piece he needed.

"I got Grieg's concerto in D Minor for ninepence here," he said, "and it was in very good condition. Then I got a lot of duets, and I found Grieg's Norwegian Dance here too. Once I got a complete copy of Beethoven's symphonies for sixpence. The pages were a bit shaky in places, but I repaired it."

Among his medley of old-fashioned stone hot-water bottles and broken candelabras, one of the junk merchants had a big supply of door numbers. They were the kind of numbers you

160

see on the doors of a long dreary street of small town houses. I longed to ask him if he crept along in the dead of night and took them off with a screw-driver. But in any case, when I only asked him how his business was going, he was quite unable to speak. The all-too-recent visit of the inspector, who had just gone on to the next trader, had shaken him so much that he could not open his mouth.

While you are not actually buying something you happen to want, you can at least have a good laugh. There are plenty of cast-off pictures of people's ancestors, usually so hideous that it is not surprising their descendants have consigned them to the junk merchants. But keep your eyes open, because among the pictures you can sometimes pick up some lovely old prints that are well worth having.

"Anybody want to buy a box of carbons for a shilling?" Yes, but they had been out in the rain or something, and were obviously too damp to use.

Mysterious whistles echo perpetually across the market. That is how the cheap-jacks warn each other when the inspectors are on their round.

"Light storage to let," was painted on an old door among a heap of oddments. Evidently this junk merchant stored things for the others if they had any goods unsold. But I believe most of them store their wares at home.

I saw a perfectly good blue leather motoring helmet being sold for 4d. There is a cheap-jack who buys all the lost gloves from the London Passenger Transport Board and makes a profit out of selling them again in the market.

It is pathetic the amount of excitement there is when a junk merchant finds he has something that will work properly. Like the old man I saw who was standing so proudly beside a well-preserved pendulum clock, and shouting out about it for all he was worth. He had forgotten about the weird collection of battered things that lay around it. Perhaps he gave that pendulum a sly push now and then when no one was looking.

161

One wonders who on earth will buy the boxes of slides with medical and botanical specimens on them, or the rusty old surgical instruments. You can tell the kind of things people are discarding nowadays by looking in this market. There are plenty of stuffed birds and animals in model scenery in glass cases, horsehair sofas, and heavy old leather travelling-trunks.

Yes, and one of the strangest junk-stalls is the one that sells baths, basins, and bathroom fittings. Some of the baths look as though several families have kept the coal in them, but strange to say, there are smart modern ones as well. I could have bought a complete modern wash-basin with square chromium taps and all the necessary chromium pipes and fittings for it, for the sum of 25s. But of course I should have had to convey it home (not an easy task) and then get a plumber to fit it.

I stood for a long time listening to a man in ragged clothes playing classical music on an old piano that towered over the surrounding junk. He had no piano-stool, so he had to play standing up, and his fingers must have been half frozen in the bitter wind. Yet he played brilliantly, and he did not look as though he could ever have afforded a lesson. He sold that piano for £1. I was sorry it went so quickly, because I enjoyed listening to his playing.

"I'm only the salesman. I'll let him be the guv'nor to-day," said a junk-seller as he jerked his thumb at a rather sheepish-looking assistant. They had rather fascinating things, like an old-fashioned cosmetic-box, dating back long before beauty-parlours came into existence. All the little bottles had silver tops, and it locked up and had secret partitions in it, because in those days they were—oh! so secretive about using make-up.

Surprises meet you at every turn. It somehow seemed very quaint to find a very new-looking topee lying on the ground among a whole lot of junk in the Caledonian Market. It was there to be sold for 6d. or less. The cheap-jack who was sell-

162

ing it also sold stray bits of furniture. He told me that a little while ago he lit on a pie-crust table two hundred years old. "The legs were eaten away, but the top was whole," he said. The table never got to the market, for he was clever enough to look it up and sell it privately to an antique dealer for £10, who probably restored it and sold it for twice that amount.

Evidently they all have their special districts that they comb for junk on non-market days. A man called William Quinn told me he drew Barnet, Hendon, and Southgate regularly in a horse and cart.

The ridiculous seemed everywhere that day. A coal-scuttle studded lavishly with imitation diamonds. And some widow had gone merry and flung away her weeds, for the weed-festooned hat was crowning a medley of old china and cast-off pictures.

People buy second-hand kitchen stoves for 15s. to £1, and Mr. Cole, who sells them, does go and fit them in as well.

One man seemed to have his junk on the brain. I told him I wanted to put him in a book, but he only said, "Is it down here?" and started routing among his possessions. So I said, "Not yet," and let the matter rest.

You have to have very penetrating eyes to look for treasures in the junk-stalls. Anything valuable is usually hidden under a heavy disguise of dirt. If the cheap-jacks knew of their value they would have cleaned them up themselves and sold them for more.

The Silver Kings

IT is quite impossible to introduce the silver kings by name, for most of them refuse to reveal their identity. They are the mystery men of the Caledonian. Any attempt to probe into their history is met with deep suspicion and resentment. Some of them will tell a story quite fluently, but there is little cause to believe it. They are all secretive and evasive, and they seem either guilty or afraid.

The silver kings' stalls are the chief centre of attraction. There are numbers of them all grouped together. Some of them are a tremendous size, and in some cases several really belong to one owner. The silver is well arranged and beautifully polished, and the pieces of antique silver have little tickets on them with details about their date.

Some of the stall-holders make a tremendous fetish about "looking it up" in a catalogue of old silver whenever anybody shows an interest in a particular piece. Most of them are over-anxious to display their knowledge, but they probably manage to impress a good many of their customers that way.

If you collect vinaigrettes, the Caledonian is one of the best places in which to look for them, especially if you want to get them cheaply. Engine-turned silver cigarette-cases cost about 15s. to £1 in these stalls, and I saw a Charles I. seal-top spoon waiting to be discovered. There were candelabras, candlesticks, George III. marrow scoops.

"How much are those candlesticks?" I asked about a pair that attracted me.

"Thirty shillings," said the man, picking up his catalogue and starting to reel off their merits.

I walked away.

"I'll take twenty-five bob for them, lady; I want to sell 'em," he called after me.

165

He probably did want to sell them, in order to get them off his stall before they were located as being stolen property that he'd bought from thieves. Try walking away first when you are thinking of buying something. It usually takes effect.

Instead of buying wedding-presents and presentation-cups at an expensive West End silversmith, there is the Caledonian, where you can find what you want for less money. There are some lovely salvers, though some of them have had a telling coat-of-arms erased from the centre. Sometimes they are cleverly altered. There was a complete silver-mounted dressing-table set in a big leather case lined with white velvet.

"It's a funny thing if that's not the one I sold a week or two ago," said one silver king who was looking at a silver teapot another one had in his hand. But that frequently happens, for some of the customers are really friends of other stall-holders in the market, who buy up some wares from a rival and sell them at a profit on their own stall.

I heard a woman complaining that the hall-mark on something she had bought the week before had been tampered with. "I've learnt my lesson," she was saying to a stall-holder, having told him the story of how she had been cheated. This particular stall-holder was evidently her friend and one she bought from frequently, but she had met her misfortune with another stall-holder. This one took it all very calmly, and I wondered whether the other stall was his too. For some of them run two stalls, one honestly and the other very questionably, and in the care of an ever-changing stream of minions, so that the last one is never recognised.

People pick up original silver ornaments in the Caledonian. There was an attractive belt made of old 1760 silver coins and any amount of chased silver bangles. Most of the bangles are not too expensive, and if they think you might be induced to buy something more costly, they think nothing of telling you the bangles are "dreadful vulgar things."

Evidently many households have been getting rid of their

heavy silver tea-trays, for there were a quantity of them about, and they were comparatively cheap to buy in spite of their weight.

The silver kings have their wares perched on one of the chilliest corners of the market. So I sought warmth and clean refreshment at Pracey's coffee-stall. They have good coffee and home-made coco-nut buns. Mrs. Pracey was busy serving the cups of coffee, while her assistant kept an eye on the stove and did the cooking. He also kept an eye on the customers, who apparently made a habit of walking off with the cups.

"How many cups have you got?" he asked a man, who was carrying four cups of coffee away from the coffee-stall.

"I can't leave me stuff," he explained.

"Yes—well, as long as you bring four cups back, we don't mind," warned the assistant. "He's had too many of our cups already!" he remarked when the man had gone.

Apparently the Praceys scarcely ever get through a day without losing several cups and saucers. I noticed they had almost given up having teaspoons, however cheap they were.

The silver-stalls really need a whole day to themselves. I could have browsed over them for many days on end, but it grew too cold and too late to stay any longer.

The Antique Dealers

You find the most surprising people selling antiques in the Caledonian Market. One of them is a Mrs. Lake, who lives at Hampstead, and who set up in the market three years ago when she gave up living in America. It seemed queer to hear a well-educated feminine voice among that strange array of cheap-jacks. But Mrs. Lake seems to enjoy being there, and to do just as much business as if she had a smart shop somewhere else.

Her stall is dainty and tidy, and she has all kinds of interesting curios. After living there she has quite a wide connection in America, which she finds a great help, for she sends things over there constantly. In between the market days she works hard in a little office in her home, dealing with a vast correspondence by which she keeps in touch with foreign dealers that she met in her travelling days.

She showed me some old glass toddy-pressers and inlaid Tunbridge ware, besides a good many brasses like old-fashioned trivets and knockers. Many of her curios are foreign ones, for she has pre-revolution Russian things, Swiss things, and odd things from South Africa. You can also get Bristol and Stourbridge glass from her, and little satin-wood boxes, needlework things, and bobbins for lace-work.

All these things she calls her "bits and pieces," and she can say something interesting about each one of them.

"People pick up a sixpenny ring and ask 'Is it gold?' " A man, who would not disclose his name, was showing me his varied stall of antiques and non-antiques. He was selling some good field-glasses for 17s., and he invited me to look at the depth of the focus. And he had an equally good condition large Kodak camera. There was a little chased silver

169

salt-cellar for 2s. 6d., and Georgian silver spoons for 4s. each. He also sold bronze figures and silver candlesticks.

"I go all over the country by car, looking for things," he said, "and I supply five shops."

I met a rather sad-looking young woman who had a carved wood-and-ivory chest among her antiques which she was selling for a few shillings.

"My son and myself run the stall between us," she said. "He goes to all the sales, but it isn't very often that I buy. I used to be at Luton making straw hats. Then I came to London to work in a Bond Street hat-shop. But then my health went, so I took to this because I must be out of doors."

At another stall I found one of those musical decanters that play a tune when you lift them up.

"I've got a genuine spade guinea that cost me a penny," the man told me, as a matter of interest. "I've still got it. Matter of fact, me wife's got it."

You come across lovely old carved wooden cradles in the Caledonian antique collections, and I saw a Victorian draw-ing-room set that included a real old conversation-piece settee. The same man sold old pistols, so if you have that craze for hanging old weapons on the walls, he is quite a useful person to know.

I found one dear old couple selling antiques, who were very charming, respectable people. The old man had pink cheeks, snow-white hair, and rather nice manners.

"We're both seventy and we come out all weathers," he said, "and when we're not here we're generally out of doors in our garden in Dulwich."

He is an artist, and had a picture hung in the Royal Academy in 1917.

"My trade is really the Leather Trade. I was a buyer in Regent Street for some years. Only when one gets too old you must make room for the young folk.

"We don't touch any sales at all," he said, when talking

170

about his wares, "only occasional sales in private houses. Otherwise we buy all our stuff privately."

His proudest moment at the stall seemed to be when "the Lord Mayor of 1934 had his picture taken with us."

There is a quantity of lovely glass at the Caledonian, and the sound of the stall-holders ringing it to show how good it is goes on all the time. I fell in love with a little glass-and-silver bucket that had an old-fashioned fishing-scene engraved all round the glass.

Plenty of people collect old pewter, and the pewter-stalls are worth a visit. I saw some seventeenth-century mortars. an old wine-can, and plenty of pewter tankards.

Drinking-glasses are another thing collectors favour because they are so valuable, and there are plenty of finds for them in this market.

The Oriental has come to the Caledonian in a stall which specialises in all kinds of Oriental brasses, while the stall-holder makes wild guesses at what they are supposed to be. When I saw him he had a Tibetan samovar and one of these Indian begging-bowls where they put the bread in the bottom and the money on top. There was an ornate brass coal-scuttle with dragons fashioned on it, and an old-time American cigar-stand. He also had some enormous Hindu gods for sale at 1s. 6d. each.

In another part of the market there are some rather decorative old scraps of wrought-iron that could be put to effective use in modern flats and gardens.

"We had a boxing promoter come down from Birmingham, and he bought one of my old ship's bells for sounding between the rounds," said one of the old brassmongers. But that was the only piece of news he had to offer.

Somebody else said that Princess Royal had stopped by their curio-stall and asked the price of something. I felt it was to his credit that he did not say she had bought half his wares.

From the way they talk you would think the Royal Family

171

pay frequent visits to the Caledonian and battle bravely
through the crowds of cheap-jacks, indulging in prolonged
orgies of reckless shopping. But these stories go round to
sell the antiques and the silver. Most of the Caledonian
traders are fond of romancing, and they will tell any tale
they can think of to try and sell something.

And the Rest

THE Caledonian is not entirely monopolised by silver kings, junk merchants, and antique dealers. There is every other phase of street-market life as well, including many of the same cheap-jacks that you meet in some of the other street markets on different days of the week.

The food-stalls are clustered inside the covered part of the market, and the roof echoes with their cries. There are cheap new dresses and lengths of material in there as well, and various household cleaning wares.

Behind the covered part there is quite another world again. The concrete is spread with pots of flowering plants and boxes of fresh-cut flowers. You can even plant an orchard after going there, for there are plenty of whole fruit trees perched up on their roots against the railings.

Farther back, beyond this miniature horticultural exhibition, there is a line of shouting butchers, fishmongers, and fruiterers. Some of the Club Row puppy-men come to the Caledonian and stand about near the trees and flowers.

I watched a man drive in in a big covered lorry and, opening the back of it, he stood inside and began to auction its contents as fast as he could. The flower-men looked askance at him, because he was stealing all their customers who were on their way to buy flowers.

"Now stay and hear the mystery man," he called from his high perch in the back of the lorry. "Where are you, ladies and gentlemen? Where are you? Ladies, these sixpenny tea-cosies—I saw them being sold in a West End store, priced one-and-elevenpence. Come on now—come on. If I'd known nobody was going to buy anything, I should never have come all the way from Nottingham to-day," he added in a strong Whitechapel accent.

173

"Anybody care to have two vests—soft as can be. In case you think they're very expensive, they were being sold in Nottingham for four shillings. I'm letting them go for one-and-threepence a pair. Have a look at them, ladies, please. Have a look at them." And he began making crude jokes about the vests, which had a very successful effect on their sale.

Jarman's stall is well worth visiting if you have a dog, because he engraves collar medals, and sells leads and collars all very cheaply. His side-line is those reins people use for teaching their children to walk.

"I used to be a suit-case maker," he said, "but when all the fibre stuff came along, it killed it."

There is a penny bazaar and a chamois-leather man who appears in Romford, Acton, and Camberwell on the other days of the week.

People spend hours moving slowly round this market turning things over, and searching restlessly for something they hope to find. Sometimes they sell the clothes on their backs and change into fresh ones in the middle of the market. The stall-holders are very patient, and most of them let people look at things as much as they like.

You can go to the Caledonian and hunt for treasures, or you can go there simply to sight-see. Whatever happens, you are sure to enjoy it.

174

How They Live

THE people of the street markets are very evasive about their financial affairs, but some of them are known to be very well off. They own six-roomed houses, cars to go about in, and have many of the pleasures and comforts of life. In many ways they are just like small shopkeepers. Some street-traders become shopkeepers, and some of the shops hold "pitches" in the street market.

That is one end of the scale, but there is also the other end —the widow with a few vegetables, which she may sell from a stall of her own or from a space on someone else's stall. Or perhaps her only stall is her two hands, which she holds out at a corner of the pavement, her total capital being less than 5s., and that possibly borrowed.

There is an amazing variance in the standards of success among the street-market community. They porbably have more than their fair share of poverty, for while they are not virtually employed persons, they are outside the benefits of unemployment insurance.

The street-traders of London are supposed to number about thirty thousand, including costermongers, hawkers, pedlars, newsvenders, coffee-stall keepers, and sandwich-men. But far the greatest number are street-market costermongers and their assistants.

Street markets are supposed to cater for the poor. Yet, although the number of poor went down considerably between 1893 and 1930, the street markets increased, which shows that they are used just as much by people in a happier position. In 1893 the stalls numbered about 4894, and in

175

1901 they were 6442, while the total number of licensed pitches in 1930 was 10,492.

One of the reasons for the increase of stalls was an influx of ex-service men, who came into the street markets after the War, and set up with their war-time gratuities. Also, with so much unemployment, people felt more and more inclined to "try their luck" at a pitch. Besides, it is so much easier for people to get to them nowadays, and the street markets themselves are so much more orderly.

The hucksters have such low overhead expenses that they are able to keep their prices below the shops. They only have to pay an annual fee of 5s. and sums up to 3s. a week to retain their pitches. The trouble is that all the best pitches are now occupied, and it is practically impossible for a new stall-holder to get a good one unless he inherits it. The street markets are very much a family affair, and most of the present stall-holders have had several generations of cheap-jacks in their family.

Some of the people you see selling at the stalls have regular employment somewhere else, and many sell in the markets as a spare-time job at week-ends and on certain evenings.

Licence fees go to defray the expenses of removing the refuse, which it can be imagined is pretty plentiful after a street-market day. Originally the ratepayers had to pay for this.

In one borough the annual revenue from stall-holders' fees is over £10,000, and in another it is less than £100. Apparently the plan of licensing the stalls has worked out well for all concerned, and most of the stall-holders are pleased with the arrangement, especially as it affords them some protection from marauders.

Apart from the licence fees there are other regulations to do with the size and nature of the stalls. They compel meat-stalls to be enclosed on three sides. Yet confectionery and cakes, which do not even have the partial safeguard of being cooked after they are bought, are not subject to this rule.

176

The different borough councils have their own special regulations about litter, and they are all very strict about it.

In the Caledonian Market, which is a toll market, the rental of a pitch in the uncovered part is 2s. a day. You can get some idea of its size by the census taken in 1930, which showed that the average number of stall-holders there on Tuesdays was about 1242, and on Friday, the "big day," 2100.

It was the new regulations that brought an end to a street market nicknamed "the rag-fair." This was in Bangor Street, and stalls are no longer licensed there, because it was devoted to an extremely unsavoury array of old clothes and junk. The clothes were exposed for sale hung over the railings in front of the houses, and junk was spread out on the door-steps. This community did not trouble where they displayed their goods, and there was no limit to the age and filthiness of the garments. Can one wonder it was suppressed!

Aldgate Street Market was done away with on grounds of traffic obstruction. This created a good deal of dissension between the local borough councils and the traders for a long time afterwards.

The City of London traders had rather a bad deal, because the City Corporation initiated a system of registration in 1911 which was designed to blot them out. All existing costermongers, to the number of 1718, were licensed, but no fresh licences have been issued since. So the City coster-monger has now been practically driven off the City streets. In any case, there is certainly no longer any room for him in all the congestion and bustle.

A stall-holder goes to market to buy his stock later than the shop-buyer. He takes back as much as he can bring away of something that he can turn over cheaply.

When he starts selling, the experienced people in the audience remain entirely unmoved at the dramatic falls of price. They wait patiently, and then buy calmly when they recognise that the bottom price has been reached.

177

The tradition of the street markets still flourishes and forms a colourful link with the past that goes back to before the days of Bartholomew Fair. Perhaps they lost a little of their flavour when the naphtha flares disappeared, but the cries and crowds are still the same. There is even a quack medicine-seller who still collects a crowd by slandering all the doctors in the neighbourhood. That used to be a very popular way of selling home-made "cures."

Nowadays the shadow of the street-clearance plan hangs over the heads of the existing costermongers. But this is not the first time it has happened to them. There was an attempt to clear them into specially built covered areas in 1893, when the L.C.C. report painted an idealistic picture of their scheme. The street markets were "to be replaced by covered markets erected on the site of slum clearances, centring round a band-stand with playgrounds on the roof."

They even attempted their scheme in building covered accommodation for Clare Market. But the traders only drifted from the actual market area and set up in the surrounding streets.

Then there was the episode of the Columbia Market, Bethnal Green, which gave even stronger proof of the coster-mongers' obstinate nature. This was erected by private munificence, and it cost approximately £20,000. "Unfortunately, both sellers and buyers preferred the open streets. Hundreds of stalls line the streets of Bethnal Green, whilst Columbia Market, as a mart of commerce, stands silent and deserted. The underground regions which were intended for the storage of provisions, and the Gothic Hall, have been pressed into service as workshops."

But what of the profits of the costermongers, which they keep such a jealous secret?

There is a greengrocer who had a stall in a street market in South London. Presently he bought a shop for £1000, but although he had success with it at first, his trade soon fell off, and he decided to "go back to the gutter." He now sells two

178

to three tons of potatoes a week, and there have been times when he has sold ten tons in one week. Apparently he calculates he makes 100 per cent. profit on his potatoes—1s. a hundredweight—and he only makes just under £5 a week all round.

A great many of the street-traders do not keep accounts and have no idea of their profits. One fruiterer who takes £3 a day, makes a profit of 20 per cent., or somewhere between £3 and £4 a week, and that is a very average income for a stall-holder. He trades mostly with clerks and shop-assistants who buy an apple or a banana for lunch. Out of this he has to pay 10s. a week for garaging his stall and stock, and his borough-council licence. The stall is out about seventy-five hours a week.

These are long enough hours in all conscience, and selling at a stall is very hard work. Besides, it does not begin at the stall. There is all the buying to be done before eight o'clock in the morning, and the "barrow" is often pushed to Covent Garden or Spitalfields, loaded, and pushed back again. The wealthier stall-holders have a horse and cart, or a car to fetch their produce in, or else they pay some one else to do their carriage for them. But a good many have to use their own legs, and only have the "barrow" to act as their lorry.

Practically all the stall-holders seem to be assured of a comfortable living, though some of the hangers-on, selling from baskets and trays, lead a very precarious existence. And they all work hard for their living.

The pirates of the street markets are the unlicensed barrow-men, who lead a furtive existence, perpetually taking flight from the street-market inspectors. They usually work under a master-man who does the buying and arranges the stuff. He takes one-third of the profits, and gives the barrow-men two-thirds.

The night barrow-men do best, for they come out from five till midnight, when the shops have closed, and hang round the stations and dog-race tracks.

179

One of them volunteered the information that he took £3 a night. All fruit was sold at double the cost price, with the exception of soft fruit, which he sold for treble the cost. He made £3 a week "spending money," clear of board and lodging. But he did not mention fines. And barrow-men usually have to pay a good many for being caught without a licence.

Warwick Street, Vauxhall Bridge Road

IT was a cold, grey winter morning, and remnants of last night's fog still lingered round the houses in Warwick Street. Some of the front doors were open, and there were lights in many of the windows, for the daylight was not strong enough to give any light indoors. A clock struck half-past seven. There was a dog howling on a doorstep because it had been shut out.

Although it was so early, there was already great activity at Mr. Webb's fish-stall. He had been there since half-past six, and is always the first stall-holder to arrive, for he supplies the local hotels and lunch-bars, and they buy about seven o'clock.

At a quarter to eight another fishmonger, called Wright, wheeled his stall into the street, and with many crashes and bangs he began setting it up. But he had not even finished preparing it when a lorry snorted round the corner and stopped beside the half-assembled stall.

"Hi! Fred!" called a brawny figure at the wheel, and Fred sprang up to welcome his day's supply of fish. The driver clambered round on to the back of the lorry and began hurling the boxes on to the pavement, while Fred called out the names of the fish and counted the boxes.

"I used to be in the building trade," he told me later on, when the lorry had gone and he was skinning fish.

"Why did you leave it? Did you fall off a scaffolding or something?"

"No—I only fall out with me customers," he chuckled. But judging by his genial face I did not imagine that could have happened very often. He said he went to market to choose and order his fish at five in the morning.

The sweetest smile in Warwick Street belongs to Mrs. Cliff, a dear old Russian woman who arrives with a suit-case

181

full of haberdashery every morning and plants it, with the lid open, on a little wooden stool. I had to wait till nine o'clock before she appeared, for she does not have to go to market for her wares, and she lives only just round the corner.

"I left Russia because me husband died and I couldn't bear being there without him," she said in her soft, foreign voice. "I've been here in England nearly fifty years now."

Her poor old feet get very tired standing in the market all day, but she always has that smile for people all the same.

Then a large, cumbersome stall came into view. It was all closed up and the things inside rattled and bumped as it was moved along. The man who was wheeling it into position was almost hidden by it. His was a cut-price grocery-stall, and he had a friend behind him wheeling some of his things on a small hand-barrow as well. Altogether he had such a vast collection of stores that I wondered whether it would be the end of the day before he got them all arranged.

"It takes me a full hour and a half to get everything arranged and properly sorted out," he said, as he unhooked the sacking from the front of the shelves and launched into his task.

The chief thorn in his flesh is the police.

"They won't allow us no room," he said, and I noticed he was making high pyramids of tinned foods on the pavement.

"They come and say, 'Move it or I'll summons you,' or else it's 'Give yer half an hour to move all that lot, then I'll summons you if it's not gone.' You see this little arrangement here"—he pointed to some bottled fruits that he was arranging in an elegant pile that stretched well on to the footway—"if they was to see that, they'd come and say, 'Move it or I'll summons you.' And I should be done, because I'd have nowhere else to put 'em."

Judging by the lavish way he was spreading on to the pavement that morning, he stood a good chance of getting some more summonses before the day grew very much older.

182

"I used to be here at half-past six every morning meself," he said, looking across at Mr. Webb bustling round his stall, "but things are so quiet here now that it doesn't make much difference coming early or not, so I come at nine. I do all me own buying of a Monday. Then I store the things in me warehouse all the week, and just bring up enough for what I want each day."

A good many of the stall-holders have to fetch their own wares from market in the early morning. The fruit and vegetable sellers always carry their own goods. There was one man who had fruit and flowers laid out on strips of imitation turf. He told me that it sometimes took him several hours to reach Warwick Street when the traffic in Covent Garden happened to be very thick. He looked exhausted already, and he had only just arrived by half-past nine, but sometimes he is held up so badly he does not reach the street market till eleven. And he has to travel all the way on foot, pushing his loaded stall.

A greengrocer was more fortunate, for he fetched all his vegetables on a horse and cart. The ones with a horse and cart usually make some extra money by doing errands for the other stall-holders.

The fishmongers' fingers looked blue with cold as they stripped and filleted their fish. Two vegetable-sellers were blowing in their hands and sharing a cigarette. Cigarettes are often shared between friends in Warwick Street, for they are not a luxury anybody can afford very often. In some of the street markets they will exchange an apple and a banana for a couple of eggs, or some groceries for a piece of cooked bacon, and so make a lunch for themselves that way. But most of them bring their bread-and-cheese sandwiches.

The stalls were still arriving at a quarter-past ten. There was a continual banging and rattling as the stall-holders set them up and laid out their wares. The early ones said they did plenty of trade with the women who ran a house for their men-folk and went to work in a factory. There were

183

several men shopping in the early morning. Perhaps their wives were in hospital, and they were doing all the catering as well as their own work.

But by ten-thirty the ordinary housewives had got their feet into the market, and were making a real business of their shopping. A pale sunlight shone through the last flimsy wisps of fog. One or two stall-holders called out their bargains. And another day in the street market had really begun.

List of Markets Described

BATTERSEA: Street market off the Battersea High Street. Open every week-day. Can be reached on a No. 19 bus from Piccadilly and Hyde Park Corner. Food, household commodities, and a few junk-stalls.

BERWICK MARKET: In Soho behind Regent Street. Open every week-day; brightest at lunch-times and Saturday afternoons. Stockings, new dresses, lengths of material, cut-price perfumery, antiques, fruit, and vegetables.

BRIXTON: Open every week-day. Can be reached by No. 2 bus from Park Lane and Hyde Park Corner. Food and household things, meat sales at five o'clock in the evening.

CALEDONIAN: Tuesdays and Fridays; best day, Friday. Held in Caledonian Cattle Market, off the Caledonian Road. Can be reached by No. 14 bus from Piccadilly. Famous for silver, antiques, curios, junk-stalls, amusing characters, and every phase of market life.

CHISWICK: Original street-traders, now moved into covered arcade under new conditions. Open week-days; Friday and Saturday best days. Can be reached by buses and trolley-buses going down King Street from Hammersmith Broadway. Market is in Chiswick High Road near Fire Station.

CHOUMERT ROAD: Off Rye Lane. Can be reached by No. 36 bus from Victoria. Open week-days; Saturday best day. Furniture, groceries, fruit, vegetables, flowers, cats'-meat. Interesting characters.

CLUB ROW: In Shoreditch. Can be reached by No. 8 bus from Liverpool Street Station. Open Sunday mornings till 1 o'clock. Mainly dogs, birds, and all kinds of livestock.

EAST STREET: Nearest station, Elephant and Castle, then ten minutes' walk down the Walworth Road. Open week-days and Sunday mornings; best times, Friday and Saturday nights. Food and groceries of all kinds, flooring, shell-fish, stockings.

FARRINGDON STREET: Week-days; good day, Wednesday. Nearest station, Farringdon. Old books, old manuscripts, etchings, and documents.

HAMMERSMITH: Off King Street, Hammersmith Broadway. Open week-days and, unlike other street markets, brisk on Mondays; best day, Saturday. Food of all kinds.

HILDRETH STREET: Off Balham High Street. Open week-days. Food of all kinds.

HOXTON STREET: In Shoreditch. Can be reached by No. 8 bus from Liverpool Street Station. New and second-hand toys. Open week-days and Sunday mornings; best days, Saturday afternoon and Sunday morning.

KINGSTON-ON-THAMES: In square near Portsmouth Road, Kingston. Open week-days, but best day, Saturday. Food of all kinds, plants and flowers, rabbits, pigeons, hens.

LAVENDER HILL: In Clapham. Station, Clapham Common, and No. 36 tram. Open week-days, but best week-ends. Food of all kinds.

LEATHER LANE: Every day at lunch-time. Nearest station, Chancery Lane in Holborn Circus. Fish, vegetables, wireless parts, fruit, groceries, fancy goods, flowers. Interesting characters.

LEWISHAM: In the Lewisham High Street. Can be reached by No. 36 bus from Victoria. Open week-days, but liveliest Saturday nights. Amusing characters, all kinds of food, fruit, vegetables, mushrooms, and flowers.

LOWER MARSH: Near Waterloo Station. A poor street market, but interesting historically.

NEW CUT: Near Waterloo Station. A poor street market, but interesting historically.

NORTH END ROAD: Just by Walham Green Station, or can be reached by No. 14 bus from Hyde Park Corner. Open week-days, but very lively week-ends. Fruit, vegetables, meat, fish, household goods, and food of all kinds. Amusing stall-holders and shoppers.

PETTICOAT LANE: Sunday mornings till one o'clock. Near Aldersgate Station. Cheap goods of all kinds; jewellery, clothes, musical instruments. Quaint cheap-jacks and amusing street-cries.

186

PORTOBELLO ROAD: In Notting Hill Gate. Can be reached on No. 52 bus from Hyde Park Corner. A household market, mainly food-stalls. Open week-days.

RIDLEY ROAD. Off Hackney High Street. Can be reached by No. 73 bus to Church Street, Stoke Newington, and then tram to Ridley Road. Food of all kinds, clothes, pickles. Quaint cheap-jacks, and queer cries. Open week-days and Sunday morning.

RYE LANE: In Peckham. Can be reached by No. 36 bus from Victoria. Lately covered in. Food, cut-price goods, and clothes. Open week-days; Saturday best day.

SHEPHERD'S BUSH: Off Shepherd's Bush Road. Open week-days; liveliest, Saturday. Food and household goods, livestock, tropical fish, clothes, confectionery, furniture.

STRUTTON GROUND: Off Victoria Street, by the Army and Navy Stores. A quiet, attractive little street market with likeable stall-holders. Fruit, vegetables, and flowers. Open week-days.

WARWICK STREET: Off the Vauxhall Bridge Road. Nearest station, Victoria. Open week-days for food and household goods.

Monday is a bad day to go to any of the street markets.

The Rest of the Markets

BATTERSEA

NORTHCOTE ROAD: At the bottom of St. John's Road. Open week-days. Chiefly food, haberdashery, and some junk-stalls. No. 19 bus from Hyde Park Corner to St. John's Road, Battersea, best way to reach it.

BERMONDSEY

ALBION STREET: Open seven days in the week; best, week-ends. Food, new clothing, boots and shoes, china and enamel ware, stockings. Can be reached by No. 47 bus from Lambeth Bridge.

BERMONDSEY STREET: Continuation of Tower Bridge Street Market. Open seven days in the week. On Sunday there are stalls that only come for the one day. Carpets, clothing, underwear, one or two food-stalls. Week-days, mainly second-hand clothing. Can be reached by No. 1 bus from Lambeth Bridge.

LOWER ROAD: Little food market. Open Mondays to Saturdays. Can be reached by No. 1 bus from Lambeth Bridge.

SOUTHWARK PARK ROAD: Very large street market with all varieties of stalls, including many with underwear, clothing, all kinds of food. Open Monday to Saturday. Can be reached by No. 1 bus from Waterloo, along Aldgate Road.

TOWER BRIDGE ROAD: Mainly food. Open Monday and Sunday for miscellaneous; Tuesday to Saturday for food. A good deal of clothing. Can be reached by No. 1 bus from Lambeth Bridge.

BETHNAL GREEN

BETHNAL GREEN ROAD: Very big street market. Open seven days in the week. Every type of stall, including food, clothing, furniture, antiques, and junk-stalls. No. 8 or No. 60 bus from Liverpool Street Station will go to it.

189

BRICK LANE: Chiefly vegetables and fruit. Open seven days a week. Brick Lane is at an angle from the Bethnal Green Road. Can be reached by same buses.

GREEN STREET: Miscellaneous. Open week-days; Saturday best day. Can be reached by No. 60 bus going to "The Old Horn" from the West End.

HARE STREET: Sundays. Specialises in live fowls and rabbits. Runs parallel to the Bethnal Green Road and can be reached by same route.

CAMBERWELL

ATWELL ROAD: Chiefly greengrocery, fish, and all food. Open week-days. Can be reached by No. 36 bus from Victoria, and is a turning off Rye Lane.

HARDCASTLE STREET: Chiefly food and second-hand clothing. Open week-days. Is a turning off Peckham High Street, close to the Gaumont Palace. Can be reached by No. 36 bus from Victoria.

NORTH CROSS ROAD: Mainly food. Open week-days. A turning off Lordship Lane, Dulwich. Can be reached by No. 36 bus to Camberwell Green and tram to Dulwich.

WATERLOO STREET: Is right at the centre of Camberwell Green. All food-stuffs. Open week-days. Can be reached by No. 36 bus from Victoria.

LOMOND ROAD: A continuation of Waterloo Street. Mostly second-hand clothing.

CHELSEA

DRAYCOTT AVENUE: Half a dozen stalls. Open on week-days. Fruit, salads, and one fish-stall. Can be reached by No. 19 bus from Hyde Park Corner to Sloane Square, and walk through.

ELYSTON STREET: Stalls as in Draycott Avenue and open week-days. Sloane Square nearest station.

DEPTFORD

DOUGLAS STREET: Open all the week. Turning off Deptford High Street. Chiefly provisions, new and second-hand clothing. Nearest stations, Deptford and New Cross.

190

REGINALD ROAD: Also turning off Deptford High Street, and can be reached by same route. Chiefly greengrocery-stalls.

FINSBURY

CHAPEL STREET: Open seven days a week. Food-stuffs, clothing, and a little jewellery. Amusing characters. Only a hundred yards from Angel Tube Station.

EXMOUTH STREET: In Rosebery Avenue, near Farringdon Road. Can be reached by No. 19 or No. 38 bus from West End. Open week-days. Chiefly clothing and food.

WHITE CROSS STREET: Turning off Old Street. Nearest station, Old Street. Open week-days, main market; and on Sundays, about a dozen stalls. Mainly fancy-work, stockings, cosmetics, and sewing-things. Women stall-holders. Very little food. Lunch-time is best time to go.

FULHAM

MUNSTER ROAD: Open week-days. Closes one o'clock Thursdays. Hours, eight to eight. All food. Take train to Walham Green Station, then No. 11 bus to Fulham Cross.

GREENWICH

EARLSWOOD STREET AND TYNER STREET: Two small food markets. Open week-days. Can be reached by No. 53 and No. 153 bus from Charing Cross.

HACKNEY

KINGSLAND WASTE: Saturdays only. Wireless parts and bicycle parts.

CHATSWORTH ROAD: Food and miscellaneous. Week-days only. Can be reached by No. 22 bus from Sloane Square.

GARNHAM STREET: Very small market. Chiefly food. Abney Park Underground Station.

LONDON FIELDS: Almost every kind of stall. Open week-days and some of the stalls there on Sundays. Can be reached by No. 30 bus to Mayor Street, Hackney.

191

BRADBY STREET: Flowers, fruit, vegetables. Open week-days. No. 30 bus to Kingsland High Street.

WELLS STREET: All kinds of miscellaneous stalls with odds and ends. Open week-days. Can be reached by No. 30 bus.

WICK ROAD: Mainly old clothes. Open week-days. No. 30 bus runs near to it from West End.

HAMPSTEAD

NETHERWOOD STREET: Mainly greengrocery-stalls. Week-days only. Turning off the High Road, Kilburn, close to Brondesbury Station.

KENSINGTON

GOLBOURNE ROAD: Mostly food. Open week-days. Cuts across Portobello Road at the top end. Take No. 52 bus from Hyde Park Corner.

ISLINGTON

GREENMAN STREET: Between Isling Green and Newington Green. Medley of miscellaneous stalls. Open week-days only. Take No. 38 bus from West End.

POPHAM ROAD: Similar to Greenman Street and very near. Open week-days only, and can be reached by same route.

LAMBETH

LAMBETH WALK: A general street market, very like New Cut. Open seven days a week. Is a turning off the Lambeth Road on south side of Lambeth Bridge. Near the railway.

WILCOX ROAD: Turning between South Lambeth Road and Wandsworth Road. Chiefly fruit and vegetables. Open week-days only. No. 2 bus from Victoria.

MARYLEBONE

BELL STREET: Mainly greengroceries. Turning off the Edgware Road, next to Church Street. Open week-days. Can be reached by No. 13 or No. 16 bus.

192

The Rest of the Markets

CHURCH STREET: Can be reached by same route as Bell Street, and is also off Edgeware Road. Chief market in Marylebone. Open week-days. Fruit, vegetables, hardware, miscellaneous.

BLANDFORD STREET: Saturdays only. Fruit and vegetables. Turning off High Street, Marylebone. Can be reached by No. 153 bus from Oxford Circus.

GREAT TICHFIELD STREET: Mainly vegetables. Open week-days. Runs parallel with Great Portland Street.

ST. PANCRAS

CHARLTON STREET: Open week-days only. Mainly fruit and salad-stalls. Take No. 14 bus along Euston Road.

KING STREET: Open week-days. Vegetables, fruit, salads. Turning off High Street, Camden Town. Buses 29, 24, and 27.

QUEEN STREET: Open week-days. Hosiery, drapery, clothing, food. Take a No. 24 bus.

SEATON STREET: Turning off the Hampstead Road. No. 24 bus. Open week-days. Fruit, vegetables, clothing, and fish.

WELLINGTON STREET: Small market. Open week-days. Fruit and vegetables. Nearest station, Camden Town.

SHOREDITCH

NILE STREET: Open seven days in the week. Vegetables, fruit, meat, salad, fancy-goods, clothing, provisions, fish, etc. Nearest station, Old Street.

SOUTHWARK

WESTMORELAND ROAD: Open seven days in the week. Miscellaneous. Chiefly food. Elephant and Castle Station, then bus up the Walworth Road.

DRAPER STREET: Also off the Walworth Road, and a similar street market.

STEPNEY

BURDETT ROAD: Open week-days. Miscellaneous. Mostly food. Amusing characters. Turning off the Mile End Road. Nearest station, Mile End Underground Station.

BURSLEM STREET AND HESSEL STREET: Jewish market. Poultry, mangel-wurzels. Specially killed food for Jewish faith. Open every day except Saturdays. Turning off Commercial Road. Aldgate Station.

WHITECHAPEL ROAD: Saturdays only. Miscellaneous: bedding, roots, plants. Whitechapel Underground Station.

MILE END ROAD: Saturdays only. Miscellaneous, second-hand furniture, bedding, knick-knacks. Mile End Road Underground Station.

COBB STREET, STRIPE STREET, AND LEYDON STREET: All close together. Mostly poultry, specially killed for Jewish faith. Liverpool Street Station, and go through Middlesex Street. Open every day except Saturday; best days, Thursday and Friday.

WHITEHORSE STREET: Open seven days in the week. All kinds of food-stuffs, clothing, etc. Nearest station, Stepney.

WATNEY STREET: Open seven days in the week. Miscellaneous goods. Chapel Station nearby.

WENTWORTH STREET: Open week-days. Mainly food and clothing. Nearest station, Aldgate.

WESTMINSTER

LUPUS STREET: Week-days only. Grocery, fruit, vegetables, flowers, salads. Take No. 24 bus from Victoria to Pimlico.

PETER STREET: Adjoining Berwick Market. Hosiery, silver and gold articles, perfumery, haberdashery.

PIMLICO ROAD: Week-days. Fruit, salads, and flowers. No. 24 bus from Victoria.

194

The Rest of the Markets

PACHBROOK STREET: Fruit, furniture, hosiery, Indian silk, linens, books. Open week-days. Turning off Vauxhall Bridge Road. No. 36 bus from Victoria.

WOOLWICH

BERESFORD SQUARE: Open week-days. Miscellaneous. Food, junk, clothes, shaving-tackle, old clothes. Nearest station, Woolwich Arsenal.

Markets Index

197

LOMOND ROAD, *Camberwell*, 190.
LONDON FIELDS, *Hackney*, 191.
LOWER MARSH, 63–65, 149, 186.
LOWER ROAD, *Bermondsey*, 189.
LUPUS STREET, *Westminster*, 194.
MILE END ROAD, *Stepney*, 194.
MUNSTER ROAD, *Fulham*, 191.
NETHERWOOD STREET, *Hampstead*, 192.
NEW CUT MARKET, 61–63, 149, 150, 151, 152 186,
NORTH CROSS ROAD, *Camberwell*, 190.
NORTH END ROAD, *Walham Green*, 37–44, 186.
NORTHCOTE MARKET, *Battersea*, 189.
PACHBROOK STREET, *Westminster*, 195.
PETER STREET, *Westminster*, 194.
PETTICOAT LANE, 1–7, 152–153, 186.
PIMLICO ROAD, *Westminster*, 194.
POPHAM ROAD, *Islington*, 192.
PORTOBELLO ROAD, *Notting Hill Gate*, 115–117, 187.
QUEEN STREET, *St. Pancras*, 193.
REGINALD ROAD, *Deptford*, 191.
RIDLEY ROAD, *Hackney*, 135–143, 187.

RYE LANE, *Peckham*, 77–79, 187.
SEATON STREET, *St. Pancras*, 193.
SHEPHERD'S BUSH, 89–96, 187.
SOUTHWARK PARK ROAD, 189.
STRIPE STREET, *Stepney*, 194.
STRUTTON GROUND, *Westminster*, 25–30, 187.
TOWER BRIDGE ROAD, *Bermondsey*, 189.
TYNER STREET, *Greenwich*, 191.
WARWICK STREET, *Vauxhall Bridge Road*, 181–184, 187.
WATERLOO STREET, *Camberwell*, 190.
WATNEY STREET, *Stepney*, 194.
WELLINGTON STREET, *St. Pancras*, 193.
WELLS STREET, *Hackney*, 192.
WENTWORTH STREET, *Stepney*, 194.
WESTMORELAND ROAD, *Southwark*, 193.
WHITE CROSS STREET, *Finsbury*, 151, 191.
WHITECHAPEL ROAD, *Stepney*, 194.
WHITEHORSE STREET, *Stepney*, 194.
WICK ROAD, *Hackney*, 192.
WILCOX ROAD, *Lambeth*, 192.

198

Some Things to be Bought Index

DATE DUE

GAYLORD			PRINTED IN U.S.A.